Frederic De Peyster

The life and administration of Richard,

Earl of Bellomont, governor of the provinces of New York

Frederic De Peyster

The life and administration of Richard,
Earl of Bellomont, governor of the provinces of New York

ISBN/EAN: 9783337732288

Printed in Europe, USA, Canada, Australia, Japan

Cover: Foto ©ninafisch / pixelio.de

More available books at **www.hansebooks.com**

THE

LIFE AND ADMINISTRATION

OF

RICHARD, EARL OF BELLOMONT,

GOVERNOR OF THE PROVINCES

OF

NEW YORK, MASSACHUSETTS AND NEW HAMPSHIRE,

FROM 1697 TO 1701.

AN ADDRESS

DELIVERED BEFORE THE NEW YORK HISTORICAL SOCIETY, AT
THE CELEBRATION OF ITS SEVENTY-FIFTH ANNIVERSARY,
TUESDAY, NOVEMBER 18TH, 1879,

BY

FREDERIC DE PEYSTER, LL.D., F. R. H. S.,

PRESIDENT OF THE SOCIETY

NEW YORK:
PUBLISHED FOR THE SOCIETY.
MDCCCLXXIX.

SEVENTY-FIFTH ANNIVERSARY,

At a meeting of the New York Historical Society, held in its Hall, on Tuesday Evening, November 18th, 1879, to celebrate the Seventy-Fifth Anniversary of the Founding of the Society, the First Vice-President, Mr. Charles O'Conor, presided.

In accordance with the course observed on similar commemorative occasions, the Rev. Thomas E. Vermilye, D. D., senior minister of the Reformed (Dutch) Church, New York City, at the request of the presiding officer offered up a very impressive and appropriate prayer.

Mr. O'Conor then introduced the orator of the evening, Frederic de Peyster, LL. D., President of the Society, who delivered the Anniversary Address, the subject being "The Life and Administration of Richard, Earl of Bellomont."

On the conclusion of the address, Hon. Erastus Brooks, after some remarks, submitted the following resolution :

Resolved, That the thanks of the Society be presented to the President of the Society, Frederic de Peyster, Esq., LL. D., for his learned and able address delivered before the Society this evening, and that a copy be requested for publication.

The resolution was seconded by Prof. Henry Drisler, LL. D. with remarks, and was adopted unanimously.

[Extract from the Minutes.]

[Signed]   ANDREW WARNER,

Recording Secretary.

Officers of the Society, 1879,

— ••• —

Executive Committee.

Committee on the Fine Arts.

LIFE AND ADMINISTRATION

OF

RICHARD, EARL OF BELLOMONT.

THE subject which I have chosen for my Address, this evening, is a sketch of the Life and Administration of Richard, Earl of Bellomont, Governor of the Provinces of New York, Massachusetts and New Hampshire, under William the Third. As the time at my disposal is limited, I shall be able to refer only to the most important details of Governor Bellomont's administration, confining my remarks principally, if not wholly, to those bearing in an especial manner on the history of the Province of New York.

As the first actual friend of the people and sympathizer with honest democratic forms of government who administered the affairs of this Colony under the English crown, the Earl of Bellomont must ever have a strong claim to the respect and regard of the citizens of this State ; and, as the unflinching foe of dishonesty in every form, an equally strong claim to the respect and regard of all impartial men.

In the first named particular, Bellomont was in complete accord with the great mass of the inhabitants, then chiefly Dutch, or of Dutch descent. He bravely and consistently defended the memory of their two leaders, Leisler and Milborne, who perished on the scaffold, victims to the implacable hatred of a small but powerful clique of persons whose only thought was profit and self-aggrandizement. He likewise insisted upon justice being done to the memory of these unfortunate men, and on the restitution of their property to their suffering families, although in so doing he knew that the hatred of those opposed to these proceedings would be transferred to himself.

A marked feature of Bellomont's career was that he disdained to increase his fortune by affiliation or collusion with public or private plunderers, although at that time no province under the English Crown offered more abundant or safer facilities for amassing great wealth than the Province of New York. His study of the affairs of the Province previous to coming thither, had tended to convince him that the so-called aristocratic party, here, that assumed to influence and direct the administration of the colonial government, was composed principally of persons whose conduct was selfish in the extreme, and who preyed on the Colony to the great detriment of its material prosperity and the peace and welfare of its inhabitants, openly in defiance of the law. His strong and ever present sense of duty would not allow him, once having assumed office, to neglect enforcing the Acts of Parliament bearing on the affairs of his government, even though some of them were obnoxious to the people; but he resolved to conciliate the loyal and well-disposed inhabitants by a determined opposition to wrong-doing in every form.

The life of such a personage cannot be devoid of interest to the general public, and must afford many valuable lessons to the thoughtful student of history. It is additionally interesting from the fact that it is more or less intimately connected with events that have stamped themselves indelibly upon the pages of history. The greatest among these was the English Revolution, which, by forcing the abdication of James II, and raising to the English throne the sagacious, brave and patriotic William, Prince of Orange, "dispelled all the mysteries of kingcraft and priestcraft, and settled monarchy on its only true basis, the rights of the people." *

* Note to Williams's edition of Blackstone's *Commentaries.*

As we are often enabled to gain a clearer insight to the character of a man by a knowledge of his family history and descent, I shall begin this Address by presenting a brief genealogy of Governor Bellomont, and saying a few words about the Coote family, of which he was a distinguished representative.

According to the records of the British Peerage, the family of Coote is of very ancient date, being able to trace its lineage back to Sir John Coote, a native and knight of France, who flourished, it is supposed, sometime in the eleventh century. This Sir John married the daughter and heiress of the Lord of Boys in the same kingdom, and had issue a son, likewise Sir John, who came over to England, and settled in Devonshire, where he married the daughter of Sir John Fortescue of that county. The descendants of this union contracted alliances with other families of wealth and position in England; and from this source are sprung the several distinguished families of later times bearing the name of Coote.

In the reign of Queen Elizabeth the immediate ancestor of Lord Bellomont was Francis Coote, Esq., who was in the service of the Queen. His son, Sir Nicholas Coote, was living in the year 1636. Sir Nicholas had issue two sons; the elder son, Charles, his heir, the grandfather of the Earl of Bellomont, entered the service of his country as a soldier, and, as Captain of " one hundred foot," served in Ireland in the wars against O'Neil, Earl of Tyrone. He subsequently became Provost Marshal of Connaught, and later, Vice-President of the same Province; and in 1621, having recently been sworn of the Privy Council, he was created a baronet of Ireland, by Letters Patent dated April 2d in the same year. Some years previous to receiving this last honor, Sir Charles married " Dorothea, the younger daughter and co-heir of Hugh Cuffe, Esq., of Cuffe's Woods, County Cork, Ireland, and had issue three sons, Charles, Chidley, and Richard." * Upon the breaking out of the Irish Rebellion, in 1641, he again entered the field, this time at the head

---

* Burke's *Extinct and Dormant Peerages of Great Britain and Ireland.*

of one thousand men. Although he rendered himself peculiarly obnoxious to the inhabitants " by his sanguinary speeches at the council board and massacres throughout the country,"* and won a most unenviable reputation by the excessive severity and harshness with which he conducted his campaigns against the Irish, he was acknowledged to be a most successful military chief. One of his most notable military successes, was the surprising passage of Montrath Woods. In this daring exploit he advanced to the relief of the Castle of Birr at the head of thirty dismounted dragoons, beat off the enemy with the loss of their leader and forty men, and after spending forty-eight hours in the saddle, returned to camp without having lost a single man.† About a year later he lost his life in a sally from the town of Trim. At his death, his eldest son Charles, who held the office of Provost Marshal of Connaught— to which he had been appointed on the promotion of his father to the Presidency—succeeded to the title of Baronet. In 1645, the civil war being then at its height, he was made Lord President of Connaught, and during the ensuing ten or twelve years was actively engaged in warlike operations in various parts of Ireland. He was a staunch adherent of the " Republicans," and received many distinguished marks of favor from Parliament. His principles, however, seem to have been somewhat elastic, for when, on the death of Cromwell, public agitation began to shape itself in favor of the Restoration, he was one of the first among the parliamentary leaders who fell in with the current of popular opinion. Acting simultaneously with several other prominent parliamentarians, who from various motives now declared for Charles II, he made himself master of Galway and Athlone, and soon after took possession of Dublin Castle.

A Convention favorable to the Restoration was assembled in Dublin, and continued its session in defiance of the orders of the English Council of State. The declaration of Charles II, at Breda, being presented to the Convention, was accepted by acclamation;

---

* *Encyclopædia Americana.*
† Burke's *Extinct and Dormant Peerages of Great Britain and Ireland.*

and, amid great rejoicings, the King was proclaimed in all the large towns throughout Ireland. "Thus," to use the language of an impartial writer, " the restoration of the son in Ireland, was effected by the same persons who had been mainly instrumental in bringing his father to the block." *

While these events were progressing, Sir Charles Coote despatched a trusty messenger to the Marquess of Ormonde at Brussels, requesting that His Majesty be informed of his affection and duty, and declaring that the whole kingdom of Ireland was ready to receive him. The King, who knew the strength of Sir Charles and the importance of his support, received this declaration with great satisfaction; and in return for his loyalty promised him an earldom, and a high military command. After the Restoration, the King, who, whatever were his faults, was not unfaithful to his friends, confirmed Sir Charles in his post of Lord President of Connaught, appointed him Keeper of the Castle of Athlone, granted him various important immunities, and raised him to the peerage of Ireland, under the title of the Earl of Montrath, by Letters Patent dated the 6th of September, 1660; this title being chosen in commemoration of the famous exploit of his father, previously referred to. The favor of the King did not however confine itself to Sir Charles; on the same day that the latter was created an Earl, his brother Richard, who had likewise been active in promoting the Restoration, was raised to the peerage, as Baron Coote of Colooney, County Sligo, Ireland.

Some twenty-five or thirty years previous to his elevation to the peerage, Richard Coote married Mary, the second daughter of Sir George St. George, Baronet, of Carrickdrumruske, County Leitrim, Ireland. From this union there were four children, Charles, Richard, Chidley, and Thomas. The first named died in infancy. The father, Lord Coote, died on the 10th of July, 1683. At his death, Richard, his eldest surviving son, inherited the title.

---

* Ree's *Encyclopædia.*

Richard, the second Baron Coote (afterwards Earl of Bellomont), was born in 1636. Of his career during the early years of his life, very little is recorded. The first mention of him in history is as a member of Parliament for Dwitwich, England, a place long celebrated for its famous salt springs, and supposed to have been the Salinæ of the Romans; and he appears to have represented this borough several years.

The restoration of the Stuarts, although welcomed by the people as a guaranty of peace, stamped the democratic revolution in England as a failure, but this failure did not kill the principles involved. The doctrine of passive obedience to the will of the sovereign, zealously upheld by the great reformers—Luther, Cranmer, Ridley, and Latimer—had received a severe blow; and the right of resistance, inculcated by Calvin and Knox, had been too successfully tested to be forgotten. Republican principles, the inevitable outgrowth of this latter doctrine, which contained the germs of political freedom, were but temporarily stifled, and from motives of policy rather than fear, lay dormant during the reign of the second Charles. These principles, it is true, were cherished only by the thoughtful few; but firmly rooted in their minds, were destined to bear golden fruit ere the close of the century. Augmented by a fear, if not detestation of Catholicism, they first showed themselves in the English Commons, which, on three consecutive occasions, passed the bill excluding the Duke of York, recently converted to that faith, from the succession to the throne. This bill, it is almost needless to say, was defeated by the action of the Lords and the King. Even the people were not yet ready for so violent a measure; and on the death of Charles, no opposition was shown by them to the succession of his brother James.

As on the occasion of Charles II coming to the throne, so on the accession of James, the nation "wearied with plots and cabals," and heartily disgusted with the constant agitations and fears to which it had been made a prey during the preceding reign, "had run into the extreme of loyalty and subservience." The King's will again became the indisputed law, and by new enactments of the Parliament the King's Council was vested with almost despotic power. Large revenues were accorded the sovereign, who was thus entirely relieved from that galling dependence on Parliament which had so effectively held his predecessor in check. Peaceful relations with Holland were entered upon with great earnestness by James, and many acts of kindness and attention were shown by him to his son-in-law, the Stadtholder.

The speedy suppression of the insurrection headed by the Duke of Monmouth, natural son of Charles II, served to strengthen and confirm the power of James. But he was foolish enough to use his opportunities to effect his own ruin. Taking advantage of the excitement attending the rebellion, he instituted measures having for their object the restoration of the Catholic religion and the establishment of a standing army. The fears of the nation— who was devoted to Protestantism—were excited, and decided opposition was awakened. These fears were still further increased by the revocation of the Edict of Nantes, by Louis XIV ; and the members of the Reformed Church throughout Europe shared the alarm of the English people. French persecution drove hundreds of Protestants to England for safety, and this leaven, operating upon the agitated nation, hastened the development of the crisis, that three years later was to force the King to abandon his throne.

Despite the growing distrust of the King by the nation, James maintained the most friendly relations with the Stadtholder of Holland ; he declared he was not in sympathy with Louis in his harsh measures against the French Protestants, and asserted that the measures he had himself instituted in England, had no other object than the vindication of his royal prerogatives, and were intended as much for the benefit and security of his successor as for himself.

The nobility of England, in unison on the subject of the protection of their rights against all encroachments, were divided into two great parties. The Tories in accord with the Spiritual Lords may be termed the party of "divine right." The Whigs, more liberal, opposed principally the encroachments of the sovereign ;

they accepted the spirit of the age, and may be termed the party of "progress." The conduct of James, who evidently no longer pretended to govern by the laws of the land, but according to his own will and pleasure, was well calculated to excite the fears of both parties. When, however, it became "manifest that nothing short of the overthrow of the Protestant Church was his ultimate design," the indignation of both Tories and Whigs was aroused.

In the spring of 1688, James gave mortal offence to the clergy of the established Church by his second declaration of liberty of conscience. The doctrine of passive obedience having been found to work disadvantageously to the prospects of the Church, was no longer advocated by the bishops; and setting the example, in their own persons, of resistance to the royal order, seven of their number refused to promulgate this declaration. For this offence they were imprisoned, but on trial were acquitted, greatly to the joy of the nation. Protestants of all sects took alarm at the conduct of the King. The Presbyterians, compelled by the firmness evinced by the seven bishops of the Church of England to acknowledge that they were wrong in accusing that Church of a leaning towards Catholicism, joined with it in the struggle for the preservation of the State and the Protestant religion. To this large and important element were united all opposed to James, whatever their party or denomination.

Up to this time relief had been looked for by the Protestants only from the succession to the throne of their co-religionist, Mary, the elder daughter of James, and wife of Prince William of Orange, then Stadtholder of Holland. But even in this patient hope they seemed destined to disappointment, for, on the 10th of June, 1688, the King's second wife, Mary of Modena, like himself a Catholic, gave birth to a son. There were many who looked upon the new-born Prince of Wales as a supposititious child; and, as may be imagined, this belief, although without any other foundation than a deep-seated distrust of James, tended to increase the outcry against him.

Both parties of the aristocracy and all branches of the Protestant church now concurred in the belief that nothing but revolution could save the religion and liberties of England: and in the husband of the Princess Mary was discerned one competent to act as the deliverer of the nation. Several English gentlemen betook themselves to Holland on various pretences, but really with the design of influencing the Prince of Orange to secure his wife's succession. Private negociations were also entered into with William, through Gilbert Burnet, afterward Bishop of Salisbury. A powerful reason urged why William should interest himself in the project, was that it promised protection to Holland by preventing the union or alliance between England and France which must follow the overthrow of the Church of England.* It was finally decided to invite William to come over to England; he demurred at first, but finally yielded, upon being assured that his wife had readily promised to surrender the supreme authority to him in the event of her reaching the throne.

Arrangements for the invasion of England were speedily perfected, and a succession of fortunate circumstances enabled William to land at Torbay, in the south of England, on the 5th day of November, 1688.† Englishmen of rank and influence now hastened to join him, and his march to London was one continuous ovation.

At the time of the accession of James II to the throne, Lord Coote quitted England for the Continent, where he remained for several years. The important services rendered by his family to Charles II, made him well known at court, and his prolonged absence was remarked. Displeased and possibly disturbed by it, for the King knew that he was a staunch protestant, James issued an order on the 22d of November, 1687, peremptorily commanding his return under pain of proscription. Thus admonished, Lord Coote came back to England the same year, and the following year entered Parliament.

A prominent Whig, Lord Coote was one of the principal leaders in the movement to establish the Protestant succession;

* Trevor's *Life of William III.*
† *Clavis Calendaria.* Vol. II, p. 229.

and when it became known that the Prince of Orange had accepted the invitation of the bishops and nobles to come into England, he was among the first who hastened to welcome him. Willliam received him cordially, and immediately appointed him to a position near his person. A few weeks after William and Mary were seated on the throne, he was appointed Treasurer and Receiver General to the Queen. Pleasing in person and manner, sensible and honest, he became a warm personal friend of the King. In consequence he incurred the severe displeasure of James, now a fugitive in Ireland, and on the assembling of the Jacobite Parliament at Dublin, he was attainted. Being an Irish peer this was a serious matter, as it involved the confiscation of whatever property he possessed in Ireland. On the other hand, this mark of the fallen monarch's displeasure served to increase the regard in which he was held by William; and in evidence of this he was created Earl of Bellomont, by Royal Letters issued on the 2d of November, 1689; he also received other and more substantial marks of the royal favor.

Early in the year 1695, William thought fit to name the Earl of Bellomont to be Governor of New York. At this period affairs in the American colonies were in a most unsatisfactory condition to the English government. The alarming increase of piracy, which threatened to drive all commerce from the seas, and an "unlawful trade in fraud of the acts of Navigation and Plantations, infinitely prejudicial to England," were two of the most serious evils, and called for immediate repression. The presence at New York, "a place remarkably infected with those two dangerous diseases," of a Governor of an unusually strong will and honesty of character, was imperatively demanded. In this emergency the King settled upon his trusted friend Bellomont, who more than any one about him he felt confident possessed the necessary requisites for filling this important position. In notifying Bellomont of his appointment, William remarked that "he thought him a Man of Resolution and Integrity, and with those qualifications more likely than any other he could think of to put a stop to that illegal Trade, and to the growth of Piracy; for which reason he made choice of him for that Government, and for the same reason intended to put the Government of *New England* into his hands."

To appreciate fully the true condition of the Northern American colonies at the time of Bellomont's appointment—which is desirable in order to comprehend correctly the magnitude of the task entrusted to him—it is necessary to glance at the causes that during the preceding fifty years or more had been actively at work in developing this condition.

Towards the middle of the seventeenth century, the intolerance and covetousness of the Puritan settlers in America had nearly cost Holland her colony on the Hudson River, Cromwell having been induced, through the representations of the aggressive New Englanders, to take steps to conquer New Netherland. Although the Treaty of 1653 interfered with this project—the Protector in this Treaty admitting the territorial rights of the Dutch—it did so for a short time only. When Charles II was restored to the English throne, the boundary lines between New England and New Netherland were still unsettled. In 1662, Connecticut secured a patent from the English government, conveying to it a large portion of the province occupied by the Dutch; and to enforce this unjust grant even went so far as to send troops to drive out the inhabitants and take possession.

The enmity to the Dutch was not, however, confined to the English in America. The British government, jealous of the commercial success of Holland, passed the most stringent laws prohibiting foreign vessels trading with the English colonies. These laws failed to produce the desired result in America, and finally it was determined to usurp New Netherland.

At the instigation of the Earl of Clarendon, then Prime Minister, Charles II, in 1664, granted to his brother James, the Duke of York, a large portion of American territory including New Netherland, to which, as is well known, he had not the faintest shadow of a rightful claim. At this time the Duke of York was Chief Director of the British East India Company, and was desirous of pushing its interests against the rival Dutch Company; he was also Lord High Admiral of England, and as such had supreme command of the British Navy.

The unwearied industry and patient endurance of the Dutch had enabled them to gain possession of such an important foreign trade, that the English were obliged to bestir themselves in order to master this successful rivalry. Public sentiment in Great Britain had been assiduously worked up to a hatred of the Dutch, and at last Parliament prayed the King to take measures "to redress the wrongs done to His Majesty by the subjects of the United Provinces." * Here was an opportunity for the young and ambitious Duke of York. War seemed imminent; but without waiting for the storm to burst, James who found his arbitrary measures in pushing the interests of the English Company "twarted by vessels of war belonging to the Dutch Republic, secretly despatched a squadron under Sir Robert Holmes, to make reprisals on the Hollanders, who had, he believed, broken the treaty they had entered into with the English." † Holmes proceeded directly to Africa, and after some success against the Dutch settlements on the coast, returned to England. Thence with a fleet consisting of four vessels of war, having on board the Commissioners appointed by the Duke of York under authority of the Privy Council, and a force of four hundred and fifty soldiers, he sailed to North America, leaving Portsmouth, England, early in May, 1664; and arrived at Boston, "after a tedious voyage of ten weeks."‡ By the middle of August, the English, in imposing force, presented themselves before New Amsterdam. It was madness for the Dutch inhabitants to think of defending the city, as the Fort had been constructed solely with a view to protecting them from an inland attack, and was useless against ships of war. Besides this, the Dutch fleet was absent from the North American waters, and its succor could not be expected. The regular attacking force of English, which alone

* Davies' *Hist. of Holland.*
† Cust's *Lives of the Warriors.* Vol. II, p. 482.
‡ Brodhead's *Commemorative Address*, p. 26.

outnumbered the Dutch garrison, was largely increased by aux-
iliaries from Connecticut and the eastern end of Long Island, a
number of whom were savages.*

The brave old Stuyvesant mustered his small force, and pre-
pared for the defence ; but the people of the city, more prudent
though no less brave, finally persuaded him that it was his duty to
surrender, and the veteran was forced to yield, although he sorrow-
fully declare he " had much rather be carried out dead."†

Colonel Richard Nicolls, who was the Duke's companion in
exile, and had come over in the expedition commanded by Sir Robert
Holmes and Sir Robert Carr, as Deputy Governor of the new
Province, now assumed the administration of affairs : he re-named
the city "New York," in honor of his royal master, and later,
having subjected Fort Orange, up the Hudson, gave to that place
the name of " Albany," after a Scotch title of James.

It is unnecessary here to enter into details regarding the rule
of the Duke of York in the newly acquired province. Towards
the close of the year 1664, the City of New York was incorporated.
The Governor and Council exercised almost despotic sway throughout the province, the inhabitants of which had nothing approxi-
mating even to political liberty. Harshness was the rule of the
administration, and grinding taxation the method resorted to to
enslave the people.

In 1672 the States of Holland and Zealand raised William,
Prince of Orange, to the office of Stadtholder. Louis XIV now
sought to inflame the ambition of William by offering to make
him sovereign of the United Provinces under French and English
protection ; but the latter was proof against these offers ; and to
the remarks of the English ambassadors, that if he rejected them
he would behold the ruin of his country, he replied : " I have

---

* James W. Gerard.

† Dunlap's *Hist. of the New Netherlands, Province of New York and State of New York, to the adoption of the Federal Constitution*.

thought of a means to avoid beholding the ruin of my country to
die in the last ditch." *

At length Charles II, urged on by the King of France, opened
hostilities against the Dutch. The opportunity now presenting
itself to reconquer New Netherland, which had been so unjustly
seized by the English, in 1664, the Dutch despatched a squadron
of five war ships, under the brave commodores Benkes and Evertsen, to New York. On arriving in the bay, Benkes and Evertsen
sent a formal demand for the surrender of the city ; and on the
30th of July, Captain Manning, in command of the English garrison of the Fort, surrendered to the Dutch fleet without striking a
blow. Having taken possession the conquerers changed the name
of the city to " New Orange," and appointed Captain Anthony
Colve—who came over with the expedition—Governor. The
greater part of the population being Dutch, the new *régime* was
heartily welcomed ; and the officers and magistrates of the Province
willingly took the oath of allegiance to the States General and the
Prince of Orange.

The wonderful successes of the intrepid Dutch admirals, De
Ruyter and Tromp, eventually compelled the English to withdraw
their fleets from the coast of Holland, where they seemed to obtain
the least permanent advantage ; and as they retreated, the courageous Dutch went so far as to follow in pursuit. The people of
England were maddened by these inglorious proceedings, and a
strong feeling grew up against the French alliance. it being openly
asserted that Louis was using the English for the gratification of
his own ambitious designs. Another circumstance that greatly
influenced public opinion in favor of peace. was the frightful
ravages made by the privateers of Zealand upon the English merchant marine. Added to this, Spain and Norway, taking alarm at
the plan of conquest pursued by the French monarch, assumed a
threatening attitude. Ever zealous of their commercial prosperity,
and foreseeing that in the event of a war with these powers, their

---

* Davies *History of Holland.*

trade must inevitably be transferred to the United Provinces, the people of England became so strongly opposed to the continuance of hostilities, that Parliament refused to vote further supplies, complained of the French alliance, and advised peace.

Charles II reluctantly yielded to the suggestions of Parliament, and calling Sir William Temple from his retirement, deputed him to arrange a treaty of peace with the Marquis del Fresno, the Spanish ambassador, who had been empowered by the States to act in their name. The treaty was signed at Westminster, on the 9th of February, 1674, and was considered by the Dutch greatly to their advantage, despite the fact that it cost them a war indemnity to England of two million guilders, and all the British territory they had conquered during hostilities. New York thus fell back under the English flag, and passed again into the possession of the Duke of York. On the 31st of October, 1674, Governor Colve formally resigned the Territory to " Edmund Andross, Seigneur of Saumarez," who had been appointed Governor.

A circumstance occurred during the first year of the reoccupation of New York by the English, which though slight in itself, was in some degree the precursor of the important though unhappy events that took place about fifteen years later, the settlement of the animosities growing out of which, formed so difficult a part of the labors of the administration of the Earl of Bellomont. This circumstance arose from the Duke of York recommending the Rev. Nicholas Van Rensaellaer "to be Minister of one of the Dutch churches in New York or New Albany when a vacancy shall happen."* Mr. Van Rensaellaer, it seems, chose a church in Albany, and went thither to assume his duties. At the same time he laid claim to a large tract of land extending "twenty-four miles upon Hudson's River and as many on each side."† He was unsuccessful in making good his claim to this land, being defeated in the courts by Kilian Van Rensaellaer. The congregation of the Dutch church at Albany refused to receive him as their minister

---

* Duke of York to Governor Andros, 23 July, 1674.
† *History of New York*, by Chief Justice Smith.

on the ground that he was ordained to the ministry of the Episcopal
Church ; and as Mr. Van Rensaellaer persisted in his claims and
assumptions, they put forward their pastor, Dominie Niewenhuyt,
as their champion. Governor Andros, of course, as in duty bound,
supported the claims of the clergyman recommended by his master,
and Dominie Niewenhuyt was subjected to great annoyance by
being obliged to make frequent visits to New York to confer with
the authorities. The magistrates and the people of Albany sym-
pathized warmly with Niewenhuyt, and went so far as to imprison
Van Rensaellaer, for "dubious words" uttered in one of his ser-
mons. By order of Andros, however, he was released, and a suit
for false imprisonment was brought against the magistrates who
had been concerned in his arrest, they being held in £5000 bail. One
of these magistrates, named Jacob Leisler, more bold than the rest,
refused to give bail, and in consequence was imprisoned. But the
people of Albany persisted in upholding the action of their magistrates, and finally the suit was abandoned.

This successful protest of the Dutch Protestants against the
policy of the Duke of York, doubtless prompted the inhabitants of
the Province to the steps which resulted in the establishment of the
provisional government under Leisler, in 1689-90.

The prominence subsequently gained by Leisler in the affairs of
the Province, warrants a reference to his career, which I venture to
present in a few words.

On the 27th of April, 1660, the ship "Otter" left Holland for
New Netherland, having on board some fifty passengers, sixteen of
whom were soldiers in the service of the Dutch West India Company. One of these soldiers was a young German named Jacob
Loyseler or Leisler, who was registered as from " Francfort." *
The inducements to engage in trade at that early period were
peculiarly tempting to young men of energy and ambition ; and
yielding to them, Leisler ere long gave up his military career and
entered the employment of Pieter Cornelisen Vanderveen, a pros-

---

* *Documentary Hist. of N. Y.* Vol. III, p. 57.

perous Dutch merchant of that day, who was the principal projector of the first three-masted vessel known to have been built in the Colony.

The death of Vanderveen took place in 1661, and his large estate passed into the hands of his young and childless widow, who was the daughter of Govert Loockermans, a wealthy fur-trader and shipowner, who came to this colony in 1633. Elsie Tymen Vanderveen was born in Hanover Square, her father at the time residing in and owning one of the handsomest and best houses in the city. On the death of her husband she continued his business, as was the custom of the day, and Leisler, who had now risen to a responsible position in Vanderveen's store, was entrusted with the management of affairs. Finally, an attachment having sprung up between the comely young widow and the soldierly young clerk, they were married, Leisler thus becoming a wealthy merchant. He appears to have been a person of more than ordinary consideration in the Colony from a very early period. In 1674, during the administration of Governor Colve, he was appointed one of the Commissioners for the forced loan; and in Governor Dongan's time was one of the Commissioners of a Court of Admiralty. Several years latter he purchased for the Huguenots the tract called New Rochelle. During a voyage to Europe, in 1678, he had the misfortune to be captured by the Turks, but obtained his release by the payment of some two thousand " pieces of eight," at five shillings each.

We have just seen that he was once a magistrate of Albany, and prominently connected with the Dutch Church in that city. At a later period he was a resident of New York; and at the breaking out of the revolution, in 1689, commanded one of the local militia companies. Few residents of the city were more popular, and it was to him the people looked for leadership when they rose to hold the Province for the officers of William III.

As shown by the baptismal records, Leisler had seven children. The eldest of these, Mary, became the wife of Jacob Milborne, who was associated with Leisler in the provisional government of New York, in 1689–91, and who finally perished with him on the

scaffold. The third child, Jacob Leisler, Jr., distinguished himself
by his persistent and successful endeavors to secure the reversal of
the decree of attainder on his father and brother-in-law; and
notwithstanding his youth, was an important figure in the affairs of
the Colony in his day.

When the Duke of York came to the throne, his interest in
the Province of New York suffered no diminution, although the
welfare of the Province can hardly be said to have been advanced
thereby. One of his first acts was to disapprove of the Charter of
Privileges which he had granted shortly before, but which he now
refused to confirm, deeming its provisions too liberal, and fearing
they might curtail some of his own rights. One beneficent measure,
however, did receive his sanction. This was the granting to the
City of New York, in 1686, of the "Dongan Charter," so-called
from the fact that it was obtained mainly through the influence of
Governor Dongan.

The alarm caused throughout Europe by the Revocation of
the Edict of Nantes in 1685, eventually spread to America. In
New York, fears were entertained that the Catholic King of
England, who seemed to be quietly instituting measures for the
revival of Catholicity at home, would possibly instruct Governor
Dongan, likewise a Catholic, to establish that religion in the
Province over which he governed. A further cause for dissatisfaction
in New York was afforded by the consolidation of all the English
Provinces north of the fortieth degree of latitude (with the exception
of Pennsylvania) under one government. This measure was resolved
on by James, chiefly as an effective means to check the growing
influence of New France (as Canada was then called), which was
regarded with extreme jealousy by the English.

This compulsory union of New York and Massachusetts under
one governor, was extremely distasteful to the Dutch inhabitants
of the former Province, between whom and the people of New
England there had always existed a somewhat serious rivalry. As
Protestants, however, their angry feelings were somewhat mollified
by the appointment of Sir Edmund Andros—a member of the

Church of England—to administer the government of the united
provinces.

The continued efforts of James to force the Catholic faith
upon the English people, culminated, as is well known, in the Revolution 1688-9, which led to his abdication and the election of
William and Mary as his successors.

On the accession of the Prince of Orange to the throne, the
Protestants in New York and New England, comprising nearly the
entire population, were greatly alarmed lest the officers holding
their commissions from James, and the adherents of that monarch
in gereral might attempt to maintain his authority in the American
colonies, to the exclusion of that of the newly elected sovereigns.
To anticipate any action towards such a design, and for the purpose of holding the colonies in safety until the arrival of the prop-
erly accredited officers from King William, a popular uprising took
place. In New England a Committee of Safety was organized, and
under its order Sir Edmund Andros, the Governor of the Colony,
whose headquarters were at Boston, was seized and imprisoned. In
New York, where the great body of the people were Dutch, the
elevation of a Dutch prince to the English throne was hailed with
undisguised delight. Moreover, being heartily sick of the continued
outrages perpetrated upon them during the administrations of the
English Governors, who had little regard for their rights, they
naturally looked upon their countryman, Prince William, as their
heaven-sent deliverer.

Without the shedding of a drop of blood, the City of New
York was placed in the hands of the militia. The Captains commanding the several companies, were fortunately men of wealth,
character and influence, and so controlled the people that no overt
acts were committed. Lieutenant-Governor Nicholson, who resided
in New York, finding himself powerless to maintain his authority,
left the nominal administration of affairs in the hands of his Councillors, Philipse, Van Cortlandt and Bayard, and sailed for England.

Before his departure, however, the militia had made themselves masters of the Fort. Having gone thus far, the need of a

leader became apparent. The militia and the people in general, unanimously settled on Captain Jacob Leisler as the person for this position ; and, in accordance with their desires, he assumed the leadership. Almost his first act was to call a convention of citizens, which met on the 26th of June, 1689. This body was composed of men of representative character, a number of whom were residents of the neighboring towns. A Committee of Safety was organized, which appointed Leisler "Captain of the Fort," and subsequently "Lieutenant-Governor and Commander-in-Chief of the Province."

It is needless to add that Leisler was immensely popular, and that this popularity greatly simplified his early labors. The Dutch residents of the Province had the greatest confidence in his abilities, and had little if any fault to find with the measures he adopted. On the other hand, he was an object of hatred to the officers of James, and to their aristocratic English and Dutch friends.

Leisler called to his assistance in the provisional government an old friend and former business associate named Jacob Milborne, whom he appointed Secretary of the Province. These two persons, aided by a Council, administered the government of the Province about two years ; and the impartial historian must admit that whatever faults may be ascribed to them, disloyalty to King William was not among the number.

In the early part of the spring of 1691, Colonel Sloughter, who had been commissioned Governor of New York, in January, 1690, arrived at his post. He immediately published his Commission, and sent a command to Leisler to deliver up the Fort. This order reached Leisler several hours after sundown, but regarding it as a violation of military rule to give up a fortified place during the night, he refused compliance. The next morning, however, he sent a letter to the new Governor, formally relinquishing the Fort. Colonel Sloughter was deeply angered at this delay, and gave orders for the immediate arrest of Leisler and his principal followers. Their trial speedily followed, and as they were found guilty of treason, sentence of death was passed upon them. An appeal from this verdict and sentence was sent to the King, but before a reply could reach New York, Sloughter was prevailed on to sign the death-warrants of Leisler and Milborne, and they were accordingly publicly executed on the 17th day of May, 1691.

Governor Sloughter did not long survive this political tragedy. He was taken suddenly ill on the 21st of July following, and died on the 23d.

Sloughter was succeeded by Colonel Benjamin Fletcher, under whom the affairs of the Province became still more perplexing to the Home Government. The ill-feeling between the Dutch and English residents, always more or less bitter, was intensified by the execution of Leisler and Milborne, who were now quite generally regarded as heroes and martyrs. Strong efforts were made to have justice done to the memory of the unfortunate men, and to cause the restoration to their families of their confiscated property; and for this purpose Jacob Leisler, Jr., the promising son of the executed Lieutenant-Governor, was sent to England to endeavor to influence the Home Government. Another cause of trouble was persistent violation of the Acts of Trade, which, though secretly and quite successfully evaded in the neighboring provinces, were disregarded almost openly and without scruple, by the Dutch in New York. The consequence was a serious falling off in the revenue—a most unpalatable fact for the Lords of Trade.

But the most alarming evil, was the aid and comfort afforded to pirates by many of the well-to-do citizens of New York, and connived at, it was said, even by the officers of the Colonial government.

The origin of piracy dates back to the dawn of commercial enterprise. In the century preceding the Christian era, the evil had attained the most gigantic proportions. The freebooters were masters of four hundred cities, and had at their command a thousand well-manned galleys. So boldly, successfully, and extensively did they carry out their depredations, that the prosperity of imperial Rome became seriously jeopardized. The extirpation of this monstrous evil became an urgent necessity, and to no less a personage than the great Pompey was entrusted the task. Armed with almost absolute authority in the Mediterranean, and with a large army and powerful fleet at his command, he eventually succeeded in accomplishing this important labor. This blow may be said to have almost paralyzed piracy for about fourteen centuries. The growth of trade with the East and West Indies consequent on the brilliant discoveries of the daring navigators Colombus, Diaz, and de Gama, in the fifteenth and sixteenth centuries, again awakened the cupidity of evil men, and piracy was revived and prosecuted as a "royal road" to fortune. In the seventeenth century, its magnitude and extent excited the gravest alarm throughout the commercial world. The practice of issuing commissions to private vessels of war was common among the nations of Europe in this century. The commanders of these "privateers" were not, however, overscrupulous in their regard for the rights of commerce; and although for a time they generally limited their depredations to the merchant-ships of the enemy, they soon came to regard all vessels engaged in commerce as their legitimate prey.

During the progress of hostilities with France, England had not hesitated to follow the example of other nations in granting commissions to private vessels of war. The commanders of many of these "privateers" encouraged by the success which attended the reckless and daring men who, acknowledging allegiance to no flag, preyed indiscriminately on all commerce; and observing the singular immunity from interference and punishment which they enjoyed, concluded to follow their example. Breaking away from the restraint of their commissions, they now waged war on all vessels that promised booty, not even exempting those sailing under the flag of their own country.

The effect upon commerce of this course, which so largely increased the number of freebooters, and covered the high seas with piratical craft, was most disastrous; trade in both hemispheres was almost paralyzed; and England, ever a trading nation, was threatened whith the loss of that which has been aptly compared to her life-blood. This alarming state of affairs became still worse

from a threat of reprisals made by the Grand Mogul, who had lost,
through the depredations of English pirates, several richly laden
vessels, among them one in particular freighted with valuable
presents for the holy city—Mecca.

The American colonies were a favorite resort for the English
pirates for several reasons, but principally owing to the sense of
security enjoyed, and the ease with which provisions were obtained.
It was well-known that several of the most notorious pirates had
originally sailed from New York with commissions as privateers ;
and it was even rumored that the officers of the Crown had connived
at piracy. It is evident that in those days the people of the Colonies
felt no very great antagonism to either pirates or piracy. Many of
the freebooters plundered in foreign parts, and their victims were
frequently infidel Moors, or hated French, Spanish, or Portuguese
traders. The advantages derived from a connection with these
ocean plunderers were almost too great to be despised ; wherever
the freebooters touched, from Maine to Virginia, they were generally sure of being tolerated—at least till they had disposed of some
of their plunder and obtained supplies. In commercial New York,
their foreign gold was ever welcome. But, large as was the supply,
it did not suffice. More than one of the wealthy merchants of the
city freighted vessels with rum, tobacco, and munitions of war, and
despatched them to the haunts of the pirates, where these com-
modities readily sold at an enormous profit. This was not all.
Many of the pirates at the places visited, having acquired sufficient
wealth to meet their desires, abandoned their bloody pursuit and
returned to civilization in the homeward-bound merchant vessels,
paying round sums for their passages.

The looseness of morals in this respect in the American colonies
—and particularly in New York—at last aroused attention in
England, and the government resolved to take some decisive action
against the growing evil. At this time the Leislerites in England—
among whom was Jacob Leisler, Jr., the son of the executed Governor—were making strong efforts to secure the removal of Governor
Fletcher, whose close affiliation with and willing subservience to

the aristocratic party in New York, seriously retarded the attempts of the friends of Leisler and Milborne to secure justice to the memory of these political martyrs, or to obtain for their families the restitution of their confiscated property. They had already failed in their attempt to secure Fletcher's removal on charges of misappropriation of the public money and general malfeasance in office, but these charges had not been treated seriously by the Lords of Trade, in whose mind the valuable services rendered by Fletcher in the war with the French in Canada, were still fresh.

Availing themselves of the public sentiment against freebooting, the Leislerites now accused Fletcher of complicity with pirates. All that they urged against him seemed to have a strong basis in fact, and it was finally decided by the authorities that the interests of the public service demanded his recall.

Never was the need for an honest and able person to administer the government of New York greater than at that period. The tasks which such a person would be called upon to perform were those which demanded uncommon ability as well as unquestioned integrity. The differences between the two factions of the Province required to be healed. The Acts of Trade were to be rigidly enforced. Piracy was to be suppressed. Besides these labors the Indians were to be conciliated and the French watched.

The King fully realized the importance of the trust and finally decided to appoint in the place of Fletcher, the Earl of Bellomont, whom, as I have stated, he regarded as the fittest person about him for undertaking such responsible duties. In 1695 he indicated his choice to the Lords of Trade, who, without delay, confirmed Bellomont. The several commissions and instructions were, however, not laid before the King until the early part of April, 1697. On the 18th day of June following, having been duly approved, they were sealed with the great seal. On the 1st of July, in the same year, Captain John Nanfan—a cousin of the wife of the Earl of Bellomont—was appointed Lieutenant-Governor.

No sooner was it known that the Earl of Bellomont had been appointed to this important post, than his house in Dover street,

London, was besieged by all those who had interests to conserve in New York. Among the number was "Colonel Robert Livingston, a Man of considerable Estate and fair Reputation who has several Employments in that Province;"* he had frequent access to the Earl "as well upon the account of the publick affairs there as of several matters which he had then depending before the Council and at the Treasury."†

In conversation with Colonel Livingston, the Earl mentioned piracy, which he regretted had received such encouragement in New York. Livingston assured him that there was good ground for complaint on this score : and gave it as his opinion that if effectual measures for the suppression of this nefarious business were not promptly instituted, the evil would increase to such a degree and involve so many persons, that its mastery would be difficult if not impossible.

At a subsequent interview with the Earl, Livingston spoke of a Captain William Kidd, "lately come from New York in a sloop of his own upon the account of trade,"‡ and recommended him to the Earl as a bold, honest, and skilful mariner, who "knew most of the men who had been abroad Roving, and divers who had lately gone out ; and likewise had some knowledge of places where they usually made their Rendez-vous;"§ he also said that he believed Kidd would undertake to seize these freebooters if placed in command of one of the King's ships of war.

It was not at all improbable that an experienced and daring commander such as was Kidd, "well acquainted with all the haunts of the pirates who prowled between the Cape of Good Hope and the Straits of Malacca"‖ would be able to cope successfully with the pirates of the Indian Ocean. It was known that few of the piratical craft were large, and that the pirates were not in the habit of uniting for common defence. Bellomont was not slow to perceive the advantages of such an expedition. The suppression of piracy in the Eastern seas would greatly simplify the task of breaking

---

* Kidd, † Kidd. ‡ Kidd. § Kidd.
‖ Macaulay's *Hist. of England.*

it up in the American Colonies, whither the freebooters oftener resorted to dispose of than to secure plunder. He accordingly lost no time in laying the project before the King.

Just at that time it happened that all the King's ships fit for service were employed in the war with France. There was also a marked scarcity of seamen, and to keep the navy fairly manned, required the employment of every imaginable means, including the constant use of the press-gang.

The King not feeling authorized to act on the suggestion of Bellomont, referred the project to the Admiralty, who received it lukewarmly and " raised difficulties," to quote the expressive language of Macaulay, "such as are perpetually raised by public boards when any deviation for the better or for the worse from the established course of proceeding is proposed." * The fact that the carrying out of the scheme would necessitate the expenditure of a large sum of money, was, however, the chief reason for its being finally rejected.

On learning that the Admiralty would not touch the project, Livingston, who seemed determined to carry it into effect, made a second proposition to Bellomont. This was that a private vessel of war should be fitted out and duly licensed and commissioned to proceed against the French and the pirates. According to the testimony of Bishop Burnet, the King looked with favor on this second project, the carrying out of which it was estimated would cost about £6000, and signified his willingness to subscribe one third of the sum. Captain Kidd had meanwhile been presented to the Earl by Livingston. There is some authority for the belief that Kidd was coerced by threats into accepting the command of the proposed expedition, but the weight of testimony goes to show that Kidd not only freely lent his aid to the affair, but even joined with Livingston in subscribing one-fifth of the estimated cost.

At this juncture the King withdrew his offer on the ground of pecuniary embarrassment. Some delay ensued in consequence, but Bellomont finally succeeded in interesting his friends the Duke of

Shrewsbury, the Earl of Rumney, the Earl of Oxford Lord High Admiral of England, Lord Chancellor Somers, and Sir Edmond Harrison a wealthy merchant, who together aided him in making up his subscription to four-fifths, Livingston and Kidd, it being remembered, having already taken a fifth.

Macaulay states, in his *History of England*, that the negociations which resulted in the fitting out of this expedition, were conducted between Bellomont and his friends, after the former had reached America. This is clearly an error into which the eminent historian fell, from a belief that Bellomont must have proceeded to America as soon as he received his appointment as Governor of New York; when the facts are, that although named to the position early in 1695, he did not receive his commission until the summer of 1697, and did not arrive in New York until the spring of 1698.

On the 10th of October, 1695, articles of agreement were drawn up in London, between the Earl of Bellomont, Mr. Livingston, and Captain Kidd. Bellomont took it on himself to procure from the King or the Lords of the Admiralty, the necessary commissions empowering Kidd to act against all pirates. In the agreement it was stipulated that all prizes taken from the French should be disposed of in the usual way directed by law; but that all captures from pirates should be sold for the benefit of the owners and crew, twenty-five per cent. of the gross proceeds going to the crew in lieu of pay, the remaining seventy-five per cent. to be divided between Bellomont, Livingston, and Kidd, in proportion to their contributions.*

It is noteworthy that the names of the gentlemen who aided Bellomont in raising the amount of his subscription do not figure in the agreement; nor indeed do these gentlemen appear to have any knowledge of Kidd, nor interest in the undertaking, beyond their private and friendly aid to Bellomont. It is possible, though, that Bellomont may have promised to remunerate them by a share of the profits ; in which case, the affair, to them, was a purely

---

* *Documents relating to the Colonial History of New York.* Vol. VI, p. 762.

speculative one ; moreover, having the sanction of the King, it could not have appeared in the least degree objectionable or illegal.

Thus began that unfortunate connection between Bellomont and Kidd, which was destined to cast a temporary but deep shadow over the honest Earl, and to bring the adventurous Captain to an ignominious death upon the scaffold.

The name of Kidd has come down to us as that of a most villainous sea-robber, and is linked with harrowing tales of bloodshed and murder, and legends of untold wealth ; and the reputed concealment by burial of much of this ill-gotten gain at various places along the Atlantic coast from Maine to Delaware, has for years dazzled the imaginations and depleted the purses of the credulous.

It is certain, however, that the epithet " Prince of Pirates," and others of similar character, so freely bestowed on Kidd, never rightfully belonged to him. His reputation among all but a few careful students of history is based mainly on the ballads—or confused recollections of them—which commemorate in most wretched rhyme his alleged misdeeds and exploits. But the ballads alone are not entirely responsible for the false ideas which came down to us in regard to him. At the time of his arrest, party feeling ran no less high and bitter than in our own day. The political enemies of the noblemen who were concerned in aiding Bellomont in fitting out the expedition commanded by Kidd, availed themselves of Kidd's misconduct, to assail all who lent him their support and countenance, seeking by this means to secure their downfall. In the prosecution of this design, Kidd's deeds, or rather misdeeds, were greatly magnified, often largely at the expense of truth.

An examination of the leading events in the life of Kidd, will convince the dispassionate enquirer, that he was not the evil and abandoned character he is so generally regarded ; and as I feel that the citizens of this community, in which he was once a respected and representative resident, can not be indifferent to his history, I venture to present, in the briefest manner possible, a few of the leading facts therein.

Born in Scotland,* about the middle of the seventeenth century, William Kidd was the son of a clergyman—a fact which of itself would be sufficient to convince some wiseacres that he could come to no good end. His father, John Kidd, belonged to the Scottish Non-Conformists, and was a man of great piety and strong religious convictions, who testified his regard for principle by submitting to " the torture of the boot"—a most cruel ordeal—dying on the 14th of August, 1679. William Kidd adopted the sea at an early age, and while still a young man became shipmaster and noted as a bold and successful mariner. His trading ventures proving fortunate, he became a man of some wealth. He married Mrs. Sarah Oort (said to have been a lovely and accomplished woman), the widow of a former friend and fellow officer; and purchasing property in New York, established his residence in Cedar or Liberty street. In the French war he commanded a privateer, and distinguished himself in two engagements in the West Indies. At the time of the Leislerian troubles he naturally sided with the Officers of the Crown and the British residents ; and, in the interests of the Province, kept his vessel in the Bay, in case it should be needed to defend the city against the French. For his services to the Province, the General Assembly of New York, on the recommendation of Governor Sloughter and Council, granted him, on the 14th of May, 1691, the sum of £150. After this, he commanded a ship in the merchant service ; and as we have seen, quitted this employment to engage in the suppression of piracy.

The several subscribers to the enterprise projected by Livingston for the suppression of piracy, having paid in the sums agreed, a thirty-gun vessel called the " Adventure-galley " was purchased, and after some little difficulty manned and equipped. As the owner risked the vessel, and the crew their lives, in this venture, the projectors demanded of the government the proceeds arising from the sale of whatever was captured, with the exception of the tenth ordinarily reserved for the Crown from the sale of prizes taken

---

* *Documents relating to the Colonial History of New York.* Vol. IV, p. 583.

from the King's enemies ; but it was not until the vessel had sailed, that they succeeded in obtaining such an unusual grant.

In the month of April, 1696, Kidd sailed from Plymouth, England, in the " Adventure-galley," with a crew variously estimated at from fifty to eighty men. Although his instructions were to proceed directly to the haunts of the pirates in the East Indies, he disregarded them and sailed for New York, arriving in this port in the month of July, bringing with him a French vessel which he had captured on the way and which on his arrival he duly delivered to Governor Fletcher. He remained in New York nearly three months, during which it seems he led a very dissolute life. It was rumored about the city that he intended to turn pirate, and that he had promised Governor Fletcher £10,000 if he made a good voyage. News of his arrival quickly spread itself over the Province, and many adventurous and desperate men flocked to him from all parts. Although no wages were offered, the agreement being that the men were to receive twenty-five per cent. of the profits to be divided among them, he easily recruited his crew up to about the number of one hundred and fifty.

According to Governor Fletcher it was generally believed in New York that if Kidd, acting in accordance with his commission and instructions, failed to make a profitable voyage, he would not be able to govern such a horde of men under no pay, who would then probably mutiny and compel him to turn pirate. *

With a complete and enthusiastic crew, a staunch vessel and suitable supplies and ammunition, Kidd sailed from New York for Madeira, arriving there in February, 1697. By the month of July he found himself at the entrance to the Red Sea; up to that time having made no capture with the exception of the French prize taken on his way to New York. The well-known and learned historical writer, Mr. Henry C. Murphy, in his exhaustive and interesting article on Kidd, published in Hunt's *Merchants' Magazine*, January, 1846, states that this voyage to Eastern waters

* Gov. Fletcher to the Lords of Trade. *Doc. relating to the Col. Hist. of N. Y.* Vol. IV, p. 275.

was "a plain departure from the objects of the expedition, which was publicly announced to be the destruction of pirates in the American seas, and especially at New York;" but I find that Bellomont himself expected that Kidd would avoid New York, and sail directly for the haunts of the freebooters in the Indian Ocean; * and indeed his acquaintance with the resorts of the pirates in those waters, was one of the chief reasons for his being selected to command the expedition.

We must now leave Kidd for a while to return to Bellomont. Delay in issuing his commission and the financial embarrassment of the Home Government, prevented the Earl's departure from England until towards the close of 1697. He was accompanied to America by his wife and by his Lieutenant-Governor, Captain John Nanfan. The voyage was an unusually stormy one, and the ship was compelled to put in at Barbadoes, arriving there on the 5th of January, 1698. More than two months were consumed at this place in repairing the vessel. By the 9th of March, the ship was refitted and sailed for New York, where she arrived safely on the 2d of April.

The reception accorded to Bellomont, by the people of all classes, was most cordial: crowds flocked to the landing place to greet him, and he was met everywhere with assurances of respect and good-will. Four barrels of gunpowder were burned by order of the City Government in honor of his arrival. His commission having been published in due form, he immediately entered upon the duties of his office. He retained in the Executive Council those who had served under his predecessors; and having administered to them the customary oath of office, he issued a call for a new Assembly to meet on the 8th of May, 1698.

The representatives of the people, not to be outdone by their constituents, now united in extending a formal reception to the newly arrived Governor. The corporation of the city, at the head of which was Mayor Johannes DePeyster, tendered him a formal

---

* Earl of Bellomont to Secretary Vernon. *Doc. rel. to the Col. Hist. of N. Y.* Vol. IV, pp. 760, 815.

banquet, at which an address full of loyalty to the King was read.

Bellomont was a nobleman of high rank, the son of a peer and accustomed to a courtly style of living—for which he ever retained a fondness; but he was not a man to neglect his duties for a life of ease and pleasure. His parliamentary experience and thorough acquaintance with English political affairs and the foreign policy of the government, peculiarly fitted him for his new duties, upon which he entered with few if any misgivings.

Some years before coming to America he had married a young girl (said by some writers to have been but twelve years of age at the time)* named Catherine Nanfan, the daughter and heiress of Bridges Nanfan, Esq., of Bridgemorton, County Worcester, England.+ By this union he had two sons, Nanfan and Richard. His domestic relations were exceptionally pleasant; and except an occasional attack of the gout, he enjoyed tolerably good health.

Wholly unembarrassed by fear or favor, he began his administration with a firm resolve to discharge his duties to the satisfaction of the King and in a straightforward and honorable manner; and although beset by the most perplexing opposition, from the very outset, he never swerved from his honest intentions.

Bellomont's fine personal appearance was well calculated to make a decidedly favorable impression upon the people of New York. Tall, good-looking, and graceful, he bore his sixty-two years as lightly as though they were but fifty.‡ No less pleasing in manners than appearance, agreeable in conversation, affable in demeanor, and extremely stylish in dress, it is not at all strange that he became at first sight a prime favorite with all classes of the community. With the Dutch, whom he subsequently declared to be "most hearty for his present majesty," and "a sober industrious people, obedient to government," he ever retained his popularity.

---

* Sketch of Lord Bellomont in Stryker's *American Quarterly Register.* Vol. 1, p. 434. By J. B. Moore.
  † *The Peerage of Great Britain and Ireland.* Sir Bernard Burke.
  ‡ Mr. Lamb's *History of New York.*

The cordial relations which it was well-known existed between him and William III, and his early aid in bringing that prince to the throne of England, and in supporting the Protestant religion, may have done much to influence them in his favor; but above all these considerations, was his constant solicitude for their welfare, and his consistent and persistent championship of the cause of their martyred leaders, Leisler and Milborne. He had scarcely been in the Province a week, before his conscientious attempts to enforce the laws and carry out his instructions, raised up around him a host of personal enemies. Each successive attempt on his part to perform his duty served but to increase their number, and the hatred thus engendered, pursued him with slander, misrepresentation, and vindictiveness, down to the day of his death; and even after that event, took delight in insulting his memory.*

From the date of Bellomont's confirmation as Governor of New York, this enmity began. His predecessor in office, Colonel Benjamin Fletcher, a man of very questionable judgment, to say the least, chagrined at being superseded, sought by every means in his power to render the office of Governor a most uncomfortable one for his successor to fill; hoping, as the sequel showed, to be reinstated to the position.

Towards the latter part of Fletcher's administration, and immediately following the news of Bellomont's appointment, began the iniquitous system of land grants, which for a time paralyzed the development of the Province, and might have operated most disastrously against its future greatness and prosperity, had not the sagacity of the honest Earl foreseen its evil consequences, and his determination arrested and in part prevented them.

Some idea of the nature and extravagance of these grants of Fletcher may be obtained from the following brief schedule of six of them, taken from the New York Colonial Manuscripts, which will serve to show their enormous extent:

"1. A grant to Colonel Nicholas Bayard for a tract of land in the County of Albany, about 24 or 30 miles in length.

History of New York. Dunlap.

"2. A grant to Godfrey Dellius, Minister at Albany, for a tract of land on the East side of Hudson's river, about 70 miles in length and 12 in breadth.

"3. A grant to Colonel Henry Beekman, for a tract of land in Dutchess County, about 16 miles square ; and likewise for another tract of land upon Hudson's river, about 8 miles in breadth and 20 in length.

"4. A grant to Colonel William Smith, for sundry tracts of lands and meadows in the Island of Nassau [Long Island] computed to contain about 50 miles.

"5. A grant to Captain John Evans for sundry tracts of land lying on the West side of Hudson's river and containing about 40 miles in length and 20 miles in breadth [amounting to 800 square miles.]

"6. A grant to Wm. Pinhorne, Esq., and four others, for a tract of land lying on the Mohawk river, about 50 miles in length and 2 in breadth on each side of the said river."

In addition to these and other extravagant grants, Fletcher made several smaller ones, the latter comprising land, to dispose of which he had no authority or right whatever. These grants also were made after he knew that his successor had been appointed, and besides evincing a desire to embarrass Bellomont, seem to show Fletcher's intention of making all the profit possible out of his government before it passed into other hands.

Attached to the Governor's residence at the Fort, was a garden for pleasure, fruit, and herbage, known as the "King's Garden," and a farm called the "King's Farm," for the pasturing of the Governor's horses and cattle; the two forming part of the King's demesnes. In the time of James II, Governer Dongan proposed to grant the King's garden for the maintenance of a school founded by the Jesuits ; but the King—much as he is supposed to have favored the Catholics—refused his consent, on the ground that "he would not have his Governors deprived of their conveniences."*

* *Documents relating to the Colonial History of the State of New York.* Vol. IV, p. 490.

Contrary to all precedent, which preserved these demesnes intact for the sole use of the Governor, Fletcher, on hearing of Bellomont's departure from England to take charge of his government in New York, made grants of the most valuable portions, probably with a desire to annoy the person who was coming to supersede him. The "King's Garden" was leased to Colonel Heathcote, and the "King's Farm" to Trinity Church; while still other portions of the Governor's lands would have been granted away, only that the Council thought Fletcher was going too far in the matter.

The consequence of all this was that when Bellomont arrived he found that the greater part of the King's demesnes which rightly belonged to the Governor for his use and pleasure during his term of office, had been granted away, and that what was left was in a most sadly neglected condition, and so limited in extent as to be scarcely sufficient to pasture a horse and a cow. The house in which he was obliged to take up his residence was in such a wretched state of repair that the rain came in through the roof; and the flooring of the lower halls and rooms was in an advanced state of decay. These minor annoyances, however, Bellomont bore as cheerfully as possible; and after getting settled in his abode, turned his attention at once to more important matters. Scarcely a week had passed since his arrival before he had occasion to carry out his instructions regarding the enforcement of the Acts of Trade. These Acts, it must be acknowledged, bore heavily upon the people of the Province, who were not only taxed five per cent. on imports and exports, but were obliged to restrict their trade to English ships trading directly with England, it being at that time well established among all European nations, that the commercial advantages of colonial possessions should redound to the benefit of the mother country, as asserted by many historians.

Moreover, as these Acts of Trade were framed by the English government, which, to the greater part of the people of New York, was alien and arbitrary, their violation was not generally regarded as a very. grave offence by the colonial merchants, the greater

number of whom were Dutch and French. Bellomont's duty was
to obey instructions. Accordingly, when it came to his ears that
an unfree ship laden with East Indian goods was in port, he
immediately gave orders for the seizure of the vessel and its
cargo.

The tardy and imperfect manner in which his orders were
obeyed, convinced him that no dependence was to be placed on the
Customs officials. At the head of these was Mr. Chidley Brooke,
the Collector and Receiver-General, who was a former *protégé* of
Bellomont's uncle, and who owed his advancement in life principally to the influence of the Coote family, to which it is said he
was distantly related. Bellomont's first investigations showed him
that Brooke was unreliable, and he at once suspended him from
office; appointing two Commissioners in his stead, until the government confirmed a successor. One of these Commissioners was
Colonel Van Cortlandt, a member of the Council, and a man of
excellent repute; the other, a Mr. Monsey, who had filled for several
years the office of Searcher of the Customs, at a salary of £50 per
annum, and whom Bellomont advanced to the higher grade of
Commissioner, at £200 per annum, from a belief that his experience
in the Customs would render his services in this new position
valuable.

But the trouble was not confined to the chief officer. Even
the Sheriff and Constables, whose duty it was to attend to the seizures,
were bribed to neglect their duty, or were themselves interested in
defeating the operation of the law. The excitement of the
merchants grew intense over Bellomont's decisive action. Mr.
Monsey's first attempt to carry out his instructions, resulted in his
life being threatened by the angry merchants; whereupon he
resigned his office, and Mr. Ducy Hungerford, a distant connection
of the Earl, was appointed in his place.

Shortly after Bellomont assumed the government, charges of
complicity with pirates had been brought against Mr. William
Nicoll, a member of the Council; and as the Earl deemed them
well-founded, he suspended him from office. The suspension of

Mr. Brooke, who was likewise one of the Council, removed a second member; and a third, in the person of Mr. William Pinhorne, who remonstrated with Bellomont in violent language for his arbitrary proceedings against the merchants, soon followed. " Hindered by his assistants, opposed by the people, and threatened by the merchants,"—to borrow his own account of the situation, the Governor certainly had no pleasant time of it; but the opposition he encountered served only to strengthen him in discharging his duty, and he proceeded no less firmly, although unsupported. His efforts at reform, would, he saw, prove entirely futile if men were retained in the Council who would not assist him in carrying out his policy; and he resolved to suspend every member whom he suspected of dishonesty.

The next great outcry against him arose from his enforcing an Act of Parliament restoring, to their families, the confiscated estates of Leisler and Milborne. It should be remembered that after the execution of these two men, their friends and adherents made strenuous endeavors to place their conduct in its true light before the English government. A calm investigation of the facts convinced Parliament that their execution was wholly unwarranted; and an Act was passed legitimatizing the government founded by them, reversing the attainder, and directing the return to their heirs of their confiscated property. When Bellomont reached the Province, he found that this Act had been treated with positive contempt. The estates had passed into the hands of several owners who had purchased them at public sale; and some of these persons had already disposed of a portion of what they had thus acquired. These new owners formed what we would now call a " ring," and seem to have had sufficient influence with the colonial officers to retard, for the time being, the return of the property to the heirs of Leisler and Milborne, as directed by the Act of Parliament. Before leaving England, the Earl was convinced that the two men had been unjustly and cruelly dealt with, although in giving orders, on his arrival in New York, that the provisions of the law be instantly carried into effect, he did not in the least exceed his duty, nor even give way to prejudice, however great his personal feeling in the matter may have been.

A circumstance which annoyed Bellomont very much, and which showed him the temper of the persons composing the Council, was the fact that they avoided as much as possible lending him their assistance, although they maintained a close communication with Colonel Fletcher, who still remained in New York.

The first Assembly called by Bellomont proved as severe a disappointment to him as his Council. Despite his proclamation, " commanding all fairness of elections and legal and just returns of Representatives," the election of eleven out of nineteen who were returned was disputed. These eleven, however, with a boldness and persistence that would have done credit to more modern politicians, managed to retain their places. The greatest disorder and confusion followed; and it was evident that nothing in the way of legislation could be accomplished. Bellomont had no inclination to imitate the example of some of his predecessors, either in managing elections or in interfering with the rights and liberties of legislators; but the manifest corruption in this case so disgusted him, that upon receiving a petition from several of the well-disposed members, he peremptorily dissolved the Assembly after it had been in session about one month.

At the time Lord Bellomont entered upon his duties, the entire European population of the British colonies in North America did not exceed two hundred thousand persons.* Of this number New York had somewhat less than twenty-five thousand, and New England about seventy-five thousand. In New York, the preponderating element was Dutch; in New England, the people were almost all English. Between the inhabitants of these two provinces there existed a rivalry which, at times, fell but little short of antagonism. Notwithstanding this, however, both moved onward with rapid strides in the work of civilization and development; and the remarkable intelligence and prosperity of their

---

* Bancroft's *History of the United States.*

descendants at this day, attests the wonderful vigor of the parent stock.

But although it is not generally known, and even when known not sufficiently pondered on, the people of New York and New England were in reality homogeneous. The complete elucidation of this remarkable fact would, in itself, occupy a somewhat lengthy address, yet, as the subject is rarely touched upon, I venture to allude to it briefly in this place.

The English historian Heylyn, writing in the early part of the seventeenth century, says: "In the time of Henry II [about A. D. 1170] Flandres was so overflowne that many thousands of people, whose dwellings the sea had devoured came into England to beg new seats; and were by that King first placed in Yorkshire and then removed to Pembrokeshire." These, however, were not the first colonists from Flanders who settled in England, as in the preceding reign many others had come over at the invitation of the English King.

A recent historical writer, who has evidently given close study to the subject, in commenting on this statement of Heylyn's, says: " For Yorkshire it would seem more plausible to read Lincolnshire, whose southeast subdivision was styled Holland, embracing a tract of land recovered from the sea by a *Dutch* colony settled therein prior to the sixth century. Boston, its chief town, already in the reign of Edward III [1327–77], one of the principal commercial ports of England—whose lofty church tower two hundred and ninety feet in height, resembles that of Antwerp cathedral, and is visible forty miles out at sea—was originally called St. Boto[u]lph's town, after a prelate who preached the Gospel in the seventh century in *Belgic Gaul*." * * *

* * * " This Saxon district, the last to submit to William the Conqueror, was as late as 1140 a refuge for the last free English Saxons. Thus, the same spirit which animated the Saxon Menapii to defend their marshes against the fearful Julius and his mighty namesakes and maintained the freedom of their native sea-land, inspired their issue in the fens of England to resist the potent

Norman Conqueror and avert his cruel thrall from their new homes. Again when prelacy and Stuart tyranny sought to impose their yoke upon another generation, the same stern influence bade them gird up their loins and cross the Ocean, far, far away to a new world, bearing forth the precious seed destined to bring forth priceless harvests." *

Thus it will be seen that the English settlers of New England and the Hollandish element of New York were identical in origin. Surely, the consideration of this fact should tend to bind their descendants together by that most indissoluble of ties, a common origin, and aid in maintaining that perfect harmony on which the cause of progress and the future of the nation so largely depends.

Following the example of England and Holland, the early settlers of New England and New York strove for the maintenance of their religious rights, but as yet entertained no thought of perfect religious toleration. Protestantism, still in its infancy, and inexpressibly dear to those who professed it, demanded for its nurture and increase the removal of all opposition; and by reason of this fact, the action of its avowed and devoted adherents in hesitating, even when greatly in the majority, to accord perfect religious freedom to Catholics, can be understood without difficulty. Therefore it is that while we, in these later days, recognize the wisdom of the founders of the American Republic, in making religious as well as civil liberty the foundation of our institutions, we cannot harshly condemn the methods by which the early settlers of New England and New York sought to insure their own religious freedom.

The fact that Bellomont signed an Act passed by the New York Assembly, making it a felony for any ecclesiastic of the church of Rome to reside in the Province after a certain specified date, has been adduced by some historical writers as a proof of intolerance and bigotry on his part, and referred to as an indelible stain upon his character. An impartial investigation of the circumstances will

---

* *History of Carausius,* by Gen. J. Watts de Peyster.

suffice, however, to prove to any unbiased mind, that it was "rather
a measure of state policy than persecution," there being a wide-
spread belief at the time that the Indian tribes were being excited
to hostilities by Jesuit priests, working in the interests of the
French. Yet it cannot be denied that Bellomont was a most zealous
Protestant, and sought by every legitimate means to advance the
interests of the Church to which his sovereign and the great
majority of his countrymen belonged, and in the preservation of
which, in England, he himself, as one of the leaders in the Revolution, had played no unimportant part.

While Bellomont can hardly be accused of favoring any particular clique or party among the colonists, it is true that he had a
warm feeling of sympathy for the Leislerians. Yet, even for these,
he did no more than common justice dictated. After a few months'
residence in New York he found that they were largely in the
majority; and, in an essentially democratic spirit, he paid them that
attention which, as a just Governor, he felt was rightly their due.
He did not proceed to any great lengths even in this. I have
already mentioned that he ordered the restoration of the confiscated
property to the families of Leisler and Milborne; and that by so
doing he stirred up a host of enemies. But he merely enforced the
provisions of an Act of Parliament, and however gladly he did so,
it was duty and not favoritism on his part.

A circumstance which occurred some months later, and which
was made the cause of many and grievous complaints against him
by his enemies, was really but the carrying out of the legal provisions reversing the Act of Attainder on Leisler and Milborne, and
was permitted out of deference to the wishes of their friends, who
composed the popular majority. This circumstance was the disinterment of the remains of Leisler and Milborne from the hole
beneath the gallows into which they had been hastily thrown after
the execution, and their reinterment, with Christian ceremonies, in
the burial ground of the Dutch Church. Out of a proper and
praiseworthy respect for the memory of the deceased, their relatives
and connections, including Abraham Gouverneur, who had married

Mary Leisler, the widow of Jacob Milborne, and who was now the Speaker of the Assembly, decided on taking this step, provided they could obtain the Governor's permission. As soon as it became known that the Leislerians were moving in the matter, a strong influence was brought to bear on Bellomont to prevent his giving his countenance to the plan. The ministers of the Dutch, French and English churches, and many of the wealthy residents of the city petitioned against it; the former, on the ground that it was likely to give rise to a breach of the peace; the latter, presumably through hatred, they being pronounced anti-Leislerians. Bellomont's sentiments would not however allow him to refuse this tardy act of justice; and, braving the opposition, he not only granted permission for the burial, but allowed a hundred soldiers to attend as a guard of honor. The disinterment took place at midnight, and although "it blew a rank storm for two or three days together," upwards of twelve hundred persons—mostly Dutch and many of them from neighboring towns—were in attendance. This large crowd formed in procession, and to the beating of muffled drums and lighted torches, proceeded with slow and solemn step through the dismal storm, to the City Hall, where the remains were allowed to lie in state for several days, after which they were interred in the Dutch Church.*

In referring to this weird affair, Bellomont, in a letter to the Lords of Trade, says: "I do not repent my so doing since no manner of ill consequence ensued, and if it were in my power I would restore them [Leisler and Milborne] to life again, for I am most confident and dare undertake to prove it, that the execution of these men was as violent, cruell and arbitrary a proceeding as ever was done upon the lives of men in any age under an English government, and it will be proved undeniably that Fletcher hath declared the same dislike and abhorrence of that proceeding that I now doe, notwithstanding his doubleness in publishing a book to applaud the justice of it and screen his sycophant Councillors,

* Earl of Bellomont to the Lords of Trade, Oct. 21st, 1698. *Doc. rel. to Col. Hist. of N. Y.* Vol. IV, p. 401.

Nicholls, Bayard, Brooks and the rest of the bloodhounds. * * * *
I do not wonder that Bayard, Nichols and the rest of the mur-
derers of these men should be disturbed at the taking up of their
bones ; it put them in mind ('tis likely) of their rising hereafter in
judgment against them."*

This affair and others of far less importance were greatly
magnified by the merchants of New York and their correspondents
in London, in the hope of inducing the Lords of Trade to decide
on Bellomont's removal.

Besides the anti-Leislerians and the angry merchants, Bellomont
had other enemies almost as powerful, and fully as vindictive and
uncompromising. These were the persons who had obtained
extravagant grants of land from Governor Fletcher. Upon investigation Bellomont discovered that about three-quarters of the
Province had been granted away to eleven persons. Perfectly
amazed at the extent of these grants, which he knew was not fully
realized in England, and perceiving the disastrous effect upon the
growth of the Colony which must result from confining such vast
areas of fertile territory in the hands of a few speculators, he urged
the Lords of Trade to confer upon him power to vacate them.
The people of Albany, through their representatives, had already
memorialized him to vacate one of these grants—that made to William
Pinhorne and others. They asserted that this grant totally disregarded the natural rights of the Indian inhabitants who had been
their faithful allies during the French war, and also interfered
with the rights of white settlers. The best part of the Province—
that bordering upon the Hudson and Mohawk rivers, had been
unwisely, if not criminally, cut off from the people by these grants ;
and Bellomont determined on having it restored if possible. After
the Lords of Trade had carefully studied the matter, they saw that
Fletcher's policy in grants had been detrimental to the welfare of the
country, in fact, had seriously interfered with its prosperity. They
explained affairs to the Lords Justices of England, and the latter

* The Earl of Bellomont to the Lords of Trade, May 15th, 1699. *Doc. rel. to the
Col. Hist. of N. Y.* Vol. IV, p. 523.

thereupon instructed Bellomont "that he should put in practice all methods whatsoever allowed by law for the breaking and annulling those exorbitant, irregular and unconditional grants."

In obedience to these instructions, Bellomont directed the Attorney-General of the Province to prepare and bring in a bill for vacating Fletcher's grants. Six of the Council were present when the bill was brought up, three of whom, being themselves large land-owners, voted against it. The other three, with Bellomont's casting vote, passed it. This bill had been purposely framed to avoid giving general alarm, as Bellomont foresaw that the opposition of a large number of interested persons would probably result in defeating the measure. Having passed the Council, the bill was sent to the Assembly, and being successfully passed there, required merely the endorsement of the Lords of Trade and the approval of the King to become a law.

But influences were speedily set to work to counteract this wholesome law. Those interested contributed money and sent one of their number to England, where, by counter-statements and misrepresentations, he succeeded in preventing the immediate endorsement of the Act of the New York Assembly. Much as Bellomont labored in this measure, he did not live to see it carried out as emphatically as he desired; but he had the satisfaction of knowing that the steps he took could scarcely fail to eventually secure the restoration to the people of the Province, of the large and valuable territory of which they had been illegally and unjustly despoiled.

As previously stated, Bellomont had three principal objects in view in coming to America; these were the enforcement of the Acts of Trade, the suppression of piracy, and the healing of the local troubles between the colonists. To these objects, which primarily occupied his attention, may be added the vacating of the land grants; and also the preservation of peaceful relations with the Indians, who were to be prevented from falling under French influence.

Unaided by vessels of war, embarrassed by dishonest and untrustworthy officials, and opposed by a powerful clique of merchants, Bellomont's efforts to suppress illegal trade were necessarily but slightly successful.

In operating against piracy he was more a power in his own person, for he could refuse commissions and protections to freebooters, and could also, with the aid of the troops at his command, arrest any who came within his jurisdiction. As his sense of justice was ever too great to allow him to palliate wrong, he could not bring himself to please the opponents of Leisler and Milborne by refusing justice to the families of these two patriotic men, or honor to their insulted names and memory; consequently he accomplished little towards uniting the two contending parties. But from his point of view he did almost as well; for he acknowledged the claims of the democracy—which was largely in the majority, so far as regarded numbers—to representation in the government; and by giving the people his support and encouragement, increased their loyalty to the Crown.

Regarding his labors in vacating the extravagant grants of land, reference has already been made. Although not completely successful, they were sufficient to arouse public attention in England to the methods by which the Crown and the people both were robbed of valuable possessions for the enrichment of a few grasping individuals. His negotiations with the Indians were, as a rule, quite successful; and would doubtless have been emphatically so, had the Home Government paid greater heed to his suggestions and recommendations in regard to their treatment.

About August, 1698, the East India Company informed the Lords Justices that intelligence had reached them of acts of piracy committed by Captain Kidd. Circular-letters were accordingly sent to all the colonial governors giving notice of this news, and ordering a strict lookout to be kept for Kidd's appearance and his immediate capture if possible. In the early part of this Address I gave the particulars of the fitting out of Kidd's expedition, and the details of his cruise for the first fifteen or sixteen months after leaving England, during which time he had adhered to his instructions. From an impartial study of the various accounts of this notorious freebooter, I am led to believe that he became a pirate, not so much from any particular design on his part, as by force of circumstances, and previous training as a privateer. With a crew of lawless men, whose only hope of reward was based on captures of some kind, which, since leaving New York, they had not been fortunate enough to make, it would not be surprising if fears of a mutiny compelled him to depart from the letter of his instructions. But, whatever the actual cause, he began his piratical career by an unsuccessful attack upon the Mocha fleet; followed by the capture of a Moorish ship, from which he realized very little booty; and an attack upon a Portuguese man-of-war which he gladly quitted after testing her prowess. This unprofitable warfare seems to have satisfied him temporarily; and it is possible that if he had been able to control his men, he would have confined himself thereafter to his legitimate work, or else have returned to England. This seems all the more probable from the fact that he allowed the next ship that he fell in with—the *Royal Captain*—to proceed unmolested, merely exchanging with her the usual marine courtesies. But this unpiratical conduct, though it affords presumptive evidence of a desire on Kidd's part to avoid exceeding his instructions, did not satisfy his men. One of them so irritated Kidd by his complaints that, in a fit of passion, the latter struck him to the deck with a bucket, inflicting injuries that proved fatal the next day; and this, the only act of blood that stained his career, and a somewhat pardonable one, it would appear, in a man completely at the mercy of a desperate and turbulent crew, forms the only foundation for the alleged bloodthirsty proclivities still attributed to him. Succeeding this event, he made several small captures, followed by that of the ship "Quedagh Merchant" valued at about £64,000. At no time in his career does he seem to have abandoned the idea of returning to England and giving an account of himself; for, as late as the time of disposing of some of the goods taken in this last prize, he is known to have set aside the percentage due the owners. He claimed afterwards that the "Quedagh Merchant" sailed under a French pass, and consequently was a legal capture. Still, if so, and if he had the intention of acting fully up to his instructions, he should have taken her to some British port and had her condemned, a proceeding to which he does not appear to have given even a thought.

Arriving at Madagascar with his prize, he burnt the "Adventure-galley," having first disposed of her outfit to pirates whom he met there, and who feared at first that he would attempt their capture. About two-thirds of his crew now quitted him to follow the fortunes of another leader, they previously receiving their share of the plunder taken from the last prize. With the remainder of his men, Kidd sailed in the "Quedagh Merchant" for the West Indies, arriving there in the spring of 1699. Almost the first news which greeted him was that he had been declared a pirate. After some little difficulty he succeeded in purchasing a sloop; and putting into it forty men and some of his treasure, and leaving the rest of his booty in the "Quedagh Merchant," in charge of about a score of men, he sailed northwards, shortly arriving in Delaware Bay, where he readily obtained supplies. Later, he made his appearance in the vicinity of New York; but learning that Bellomont was in Boston, he proceeded to Rhode Island, where he disembarked a messenger to inform the Earl of his arrival, and to make protestations of his innocence.

Bellomont was overjoyed to hear that Kidd was so near at hand and resolved to capture him, as his reputation in England was beginning to suffer from his connection with the expedition. With the advice of his Massachusetts Council, he sent back word to Kidd that if his representations were true he could come to Boston with safety.

On the 1st of July, 1699, Kidd arrived in Boston in his sloop, and presented himself before the Governor and his Council for examination. He was not successful in making his innocence appear, but the Earl hoping to discover where the ship "Quedagh Merchant" was secreted, refrained from committing him to prison. A number of circumstances, however, showed Bellomont that the temper of the people of the Province was favorable to Kidd, and

48

LIFE AND ADMINISTRATION OF

fearing his escape and the disappearance of his spoil, he gave orders, on the 6th of July, for his arrest. At the same time, the cargo was taken possession of by commissioners appointed by the Council, and a search was instituted for such goods and treasure as had been concealed or disposed of by Kidd, in the several places where he had touched before arriving at Boston.

After his arrest, Kidd sent word to Bellomont that if he "would let him go to the place where he left the 'Quedagh Merchant,' and to St. Thomas's Island and Curaçao, he would undertake to bring off fifty or three score thousand pounds which would otherwise be lost:" and, "that he would be satisfied to goe a Prisoner."*

Situated as Bellomont was, he did not dare to entertain this proposal; but after trying in vain to learn where the "Quedagh Merchant" lay, he ordered a vessel to be fitted out to go in search of her. Before this vessel sailed, however, he received information from a reliable source that the men left in charge of the "Quedagh Merchant," had removed her cargo in a sloop to Curaçao, and then burnt her to the water's edge.

The commissioners appointed to take charge of the property of Kidd, reported the total of all seized and recovered as "one thousand one hundred and eleven ounces of gold, two thousand three hundred and fifty three ounces of silver, fifty-seven bags of sugar, forty-one bales of goods, and seventeen pieces of canvas." A portion of this property consisted of several pieces of plate and two hundred and sixty dollars in money belonging to Mrs. Kidd; and twenty-five crowns, English money, belonging to her maid; all of which was subsequently restored.

It having been decided to try Kidd in London, the Home Government, sent over the Advice Frigate, commanded by Captain Wynn, to bring him thither; and, in company with thirty other pirates, he arrived in England on the 12th of April, 1700, and was committed to prison in London. A year passed before he was brought to trial. In the meantime a fierce political opposition to

*The Earl of Bellomont to the Lords of Trade, Jan. 5th, 1699. *Doc. rel. to Col. Hist. of N. Y.* Vol. IV, p. 602.

Lord Somers and the Earl of Oxford, respectively Lord Chancellor
and Lord High Admiral of England, had sprung up, and their
impeachment was determined upon. Every means was taken by
their enemies to effect their ruin ; and among other charges brought
against them, was that of connection with Captain Kidd, in which
the Earl of Bellomont also was mentioned.

The enemies of Bellomont in England, principal among
whom were the agents of those he had offended by his activity in
suppressing illegal trade and in vacating the land grants, took
advantage of this affair to press for his removal from office. They
insinuated that he was sent from New York to countenance Kidd
and other pirates, in the face of the fact that he had been the means
of causing the arrest of a number of freebooters, and that he had
almost succeeded in eradicating the evil in the provinces over
which he governed, and that, too, by his vigorous and unaided
measures.

At this time also, the question of the Irish forfeitures was in
agitation in Parliament, and much opposition was shown to the
grants of confiscated estates made by William III to several of his
favorites. The efforts of the Tories and Republicans—who united
against the Whigs—were successful ; and in abolishing the grants
no distinction was made between those who were enriched by
"injudicious partiality" and those who had been "sparingly
rewarded" for services to the State and the Protestant religion.
Among those who suffered was Bellomont, who found himself
deprived of an estate to which he was entitled as well by reason of
the services of his father and grandfather, as by his own zeal in
supporting the King, and the losses he was at by the rebellion in
Ireland.

The malicious rumors regarding his complicity with pirates,
and the proceedings in relation to this and other matters in the
House of Commons—where his name was now frequently dragged
into debate—annoyed and worried him exceedingly. Conscious of
his entire innocence of evil design, and knowing how earnestly he
strove to discharge his onerous duties to the satisfaction of his

sovereign, his sorrow and mortification at being thus grossly maligned and misrepresented must have been keen in the extreme. But his proud nature, while chafing under this harsh and unjust persecution and neglect, gave way to but little complaint; nor did he for an instant relax that stern attention to duty which with him was ever a fixed principle. The following extract from a communication by him to the Lords of Trade, dated October 17th, 1700, shows the temperate nature of his remonstrances against the treatment he was receiving:

" I have been much troubled to find my name brought on the stage of the House of Commons about Kidd. 'Twas hard I thought I should be push'd at so vehemently when it was known I had taken Kidd and secur'd him in order to his punishment; which was a sure sign the noble Lords concern'd with me, and myself, had no criminal design in setting out that ship. Another mortification I have met with is the loss of a rent-charge of a £1,000 a year which the King was pleased to give me upon an Irish forfeited estate, in recompense of the great loss I had sustained by the rebellion in Ireland. If I have served the King and interests of England here, I am sure I have been strangely rewarded there."

All through his administration Bellomont showed himself possessed of an inflexible integrity. By winking at illegal trade he could easily have gained the favor of the merchants, and silenced all opposition; for the clamor against him arose mainly from the fact that many of those engaged in trade found their profits sadly lessened by his extraordinary vigilance; by becoming a partner in their unlawful practices he could quietly, but surely, have amassed a fortune. But he pursued an exactly opposite course; and so careful was he not to involve himself in any way with those engaged in commercial transactions, where it was possible that the influence of his name might be used in evading the law, that he refused an offer of silent partnership in a legitimate business, made to him by a New England merchant.* He might have added largely to his

---

* The Earl of Bellomont to the Lords of Trade, 28th Nov., 1700. *Doc. relating to Col. Hist. N. Y.* Vol. IV, p. 792.

income by granting immunity or protection to pirates; but though very tempting inducements were held out to him—amounting in one instance at least to £5000, for protecting a single company of pirates,* and in several other instances to quite large sums for similar services, he indignantly refused them all.

Having taken Kidd into custody, he carefully guarded all the treasure seized with him, and instituted an honest search for what had been removed from the sloop before it put into Boston. Having recovered this portion, he added it to the original seizure and sent the whole to England, "without retaining to the value of a farthing" for himself; and, according to the testimony of Secretary Vernon,† he pursued the same honest course with the effects of every pirate he seized.

Bellomont's own statement in regard to the possibilities of profit in administering the government of New York, shows that the post could have been made a decidedly valuable one to a Governor with an elastic conscience. He says: "'Tis true if I could make this a mart of piracy, confederate with the merchants and wink at their unlawful trade; if I would pocket all the off-reckonings, make three hundred pounds per annum of the article of victualling the poor soldiers, muster half Companies, pack an Assembly that would give me what money I pleased and let me misapply it as I pleased, and pocket a great part of the publick moneys; I could make this government very valuable, I believe more than that of Ireland, which is reckoned the best government in his Majestie's gift." ‡

But the honest Bellomont refused to profit by doing wrong himself, or allowing others to do wrong. He contented himself therefore with his legitimate perquisites, an account of which for the first year of his administration in this Province, with a reference to his salary, I quote from one of his letters to the Lords of Trade:

"That your Lordships may be judges of all the profits of this

---

*Doc. relating to the Colonial Hist. of the State of New York. Vol. IV, p. 458.
† Letters of James Vernon to the Duke of Shrewsbury. Vol. III, p. 27.
‡ Doc relating to the Colonial History of the State of New York. Vol. IV, p. 378.

government, I resolve you shall know to a shilling what the perquisites are from time to time. I formerly sent you an account of the seizures of ships and unlawful goods with the apprizements and sales of them, and for how much; and in thirteen months that I have been here I have got but eighty-three pounds six shillings New York money from the Secretary for passes for Ships, Licenses for Marriages and Probats of Wills and all other things wherein the Scale of the Province has been used. And when I went to Albany the present from the Indians consisting in Beaver skins and some few others skins, I sold for eighty pounds nine shillings and ten pence New York money. I can safely declare upon oath that the particulars above specifyed and my salary of four hundred pounds *per annum* are all the profits I have had, received, or made directly or indirectly since my being in the Government, that I know or remember." *

When Kidd was brought before the Commissioners in England, he defended himself on the ground that his men had forced him to exceed his instructions. When questioned as to the amount of treasure brought by him to New England, he said he estimated it to be worth about £30,000; but added that part of it had been embezzled by those who got it into their hands, although he acquitted Lord Bellomont of having kept any part of it.

The trial of Kidd did not take place until the 8th of May, 1701. Having been "found guilty on an indictment for the murder of Moore, the gunner, and on five separate indictments for piracy, he was sentenced to be hung, and in the same month [May 12th] was accordingly executed." †

Some apologists for Kidd, in their endeavor to make it appear that he was a martyr to circumstances, have felt it necessary to blacken the character of Bellomont, whom they accuse of dealing perfidiously with his former friend. A conscientious study of the whole subject must however convince the impartial and unprejudiced student that no other course was open to an honest man like

* *Doc. relating to the Colonial History of the State of New York.* Vol. VI, p. 522.
† Henry C. Murphy.

Bellomont, than that which he took. His duty as a magistrate was plain; he had orders to suppress piracy and to arrest pirates; and so far as he had the power he carried out the law. Even if Kidd had been forced into piracy by a mutinous crew, it was not for Bellomont to decide that he was not guilty. His duty to himself and to his family demanded that he should exonerate himself from all charges of complicity with Kidd's illegal deeds; and this was only possible through the fullest investigation—which, to his credit be it said, he anxiously courted.

"To an intelligent and candid judge of human actions," says the eminently wise Macaulay, from whom I quote, "it will not appear that any of the persons at whose expense the "Adventure-galley" was fitted out deserved serious blame. The worst that could be imputed even to Bellomont, who had drawn in all the rest, was that he had been led into a fault by his ardent zeal for the public service and by the generosity of a nature as little prone to suspect as to devise villainies. His friends * * * might surely be pardoned for giving credit to his recommendation. It his highly probable that the motives which induced some of them to aid his design was genuine public spirit. But if we suppose them to have had a view to gain, it was to legitimate gain. Their conduct was the very opposite of corrupt. Not only had they taken no money, they had disbursed money largely and had disbursed it with the certainty that they should never be reimbursed unless the outlay proved beneficial to the public. That they meant well they proved by staking thousands on the success of their plan; and if they erred in judgment the loss of those thousands was surely a sufficient punishment for such an error. On this subject there would probably have been no difference of opinion had not Somers been one of the contributors."*

I have thus far merely attempted to show the obstacles encountered by Bellomont in his attempts to suppress piracy and illegal trade; and have dwelt briefly on the opposition awakened by

* *History of England.*

his labors in this direction and against the extravagant land grants. These labors were the most important of his administration, and to them he gave the greater part of his attention and energy. His success, it is true, was far from being what was expected by the English government or desired by himself. Yet, in the face of all the circumstances, it was as much as could have been accomplished by an impartial and honest governor. At the time he came to the Province, knavery and rascality may be said to have been at a premium, and those who practised them unblushingly, became, in many instances, both wealthy and powerful. This element, with the friends and adherents of Fletcher and the so-called " Jacobites "— who detested Bellomont for his efforts in furthering the English Revolution—formed a party which not only steadily opposed every reform introduced by the new Governor, but also persistently misrepresented and maligned him. Active in the Province, it had also its agents in England : and with a spirit similar to that which actuates some of our modern political parties, it seems that their rallying cry was " anything to beat " Bellomont. It is impossible to say how far their attempts would have been successful, had not the hand of death intervened and removed the object of their persecutions.

The time allotted to the delivery of this Address does not permit of my touching on any of the minor matters that engaged Bellomont's attention in his government of this Province ; and for the same reason I am obliged to omit any account of his administration in England. One subject, however, I feel that simple justice demands I should not wholly neglect. Therefore I shall detain you a few minutes longer to refer to his religious character, which was variously assailed by his enemies, and with such success as to lead the Bishops of London to congratulate the Reverend Mr. Vesey, Rector of Trinity Church, on the probable success of the efforts made for the Earl's removal from office.

Although but little is known of the religious tendencies of Bellomont in early life, it is certain that in his later years he was a professing Christian, and a regular attendant at church and communion. There can be no more question of his sincerity than that of thousands of worthy persons who in youth have not been especially noted for their religious zeal, but who in mature life become pillars of virtue and piety. In New York he was attentive to his religious duties and zealous in promoting Christianity, particularly among the Indians.

Bellomont's neglect in attending church began about the time the Act of Assembly was passed vacating the extravagant land grants. Among those who became his enemies, owing to his efforts in favor of this act, was the Reverend Godfrey Dellius, the Dutch minister at Albany. This person, by adopting the methods then in vogue for obtaining lands from the Indians, became possessed of an immense tract of land, described as covering eight hundred and forty square miles, which was duly granted to him by Governor Fletcher. The evil of these land grants was clearly perceived by the Assembly and the conduct of those who obtaind them justly denounced. The course of Dellius seems to have been deemed peculiarly reprehensible, he being a clergyman ; and when the Bill vacating the grants was sent to the Assembly, that body attached to it a clause for depriving him of his benefice at Albany, and refused to pass the Bill without that clause. To this Bellomont and his Council agreed, believing that it was " better to lose a wicked Clergyman than a good Bill."

Shortly after the passage of this Act those persons who were deprived of land by it, subscribed £700, and employed Dellius to represent them in England. Fortified with certificates of piety and good life, the latter went abroad, and succeeded in prejudicing in his favor the Classes of Amsterdam, which sent Bellomont a remonstrance. In England he was no less successful. The Bishops of London, who, it appears, had then jurisdiction over New York, likewise hearkened to his representations of Bellomont, and came to regard the Earl as a personage dangerous alike to church and state. This opinion was strengthened by a communication from the Wardens and Vestry of Trinity Church, which represented Bellomont as the enemy of that Church, and prayed that the

Bishop would interest himself in protecting it from the destruction threatened. The only step taken by the Earl against Trinity Church was to approve of the Act which deprived it of the King's Farm granted to it by Governor Fletcher; and this proceeding was by no means harsh, for in it Bellomont but reclaimed land rightfully belonging to the Governor's house, and for which he had pressing need, as I have previously stated.

It is strange that merely depriving the Church of a piece of land, to which it had but seven years' lease, should have sufficed to obliterate the recollection of Bellomont's numerous benefactions and kindnesses of a previous date. But such was the case. Mr. Vesey, the clergyman to whom Bellomont had been a good friend, now became his enemy, and not only neglected to pray for him, as was the custom towards all Governors, but openly and repeatedly prayed for the safe passage and success of Dellius, who had been deprived by law of his benefice and had gone abroad the avowed enemy of the Earl. It can scarcely be wondered at that Bellomont remained away from church under the circumstances. That he did not abandon his religious duties and that he did not become an enemy of the church, is evident from the regularity of his attendance at King's Chapel in Boston, and the solicitude he manifested for the welfare of religion in that place.

Bellomont's visit to Massachusetts took place in 1699. In the spring of that year, having succeeded in restoring the affairs of New York to a reasonable degree of order, he accepted the invitation of the Lieutenant-Governor, Council and Assembly of Massachusetts, to visit that Province. Leaving the government of New York in the hands of Lieutenant-Governor Nanfan, he departed for Boston, accompanied by Lady Bellomont and a large retinue of servants.

I have not time to dwell, even briefly, on Bellomont's course in New England. He was everywhere well received by the inhabitants, who were greatly pleased with him. His various duties in Massachusetts and New Hampshire occupied his attention during the remainder of the year, and in that time he was the recipient of the sum of £1500, voted him by the General Court of Massachusetts, with which he was in perfect harmony. A most important incident of his sojourn in New England, was the arrest of Captain Kidd, the details of which I have already given.

Returning to New York at the close of the year, he resumed his old battle against illegal trade and piracy, and gave those who persisted in violating the laws so little peace, that a petition against him, signed by a large number of New York merchants, was sent to England. It contained thirty-two heads of complaint, and charged Bellomont with defaming the character of eminent and respectable persons, by accusing them of corrupt practices in trade, and with abetting piracy. About the same time, the merchants of London petitioned the King to interfere and afford redress to their suffering brethren in New York. Despite these assaults, Bellomont gave them no peace, so long as he suspected they were violating the law ; and to my mind no greater proof of his honesty could be adduced than this fact.

The continual worry and annoyance to which he was subjected by his numerous enemies, both in America and England, had a bad effect on his general health ; and in consequence, the gout, which had lately begun to give him serious trouble, made rapid headway. In February, 1701, an unusually severe attack set in, which terminated fatally, on the 5th of March following, producing a profound feeling of grief in the provinces.

The remains of the Earl were interred with becoming honors "in the chapel of the Fort at the Battery,"* " then occupied by the royal military forces for public worship."† When the Fort was taken down and the Battery leveled, the leaden coffin was removed, and finally deposited in St. Paul's Churchyard. Dunlap, the historian, cites Mr. Pintard as authority for the statement that this Society, at one time, possessed the Earl's coffin-plate.

* Sketch of Lord Bellomont, by J. B. Moore ; in Stryker's *Amer. Quar. Register*, Vol. I.

† Discourse (August, 1856) by the Rev. Dr. Thomas DeWitt.

In Massachusetts, the general grief was no less profound than in New York, and a general fast was ordered throughout that Province.

Lady Bellomont remained in New York for several years after her husband's death; but finally went to live in England, where she married a gentleman named Samuel Pytts. She survived the Earl some thirty-six years.

At the time of Bellomont's death, Lieutenant-Governor Nanfan was absent in Barbadoes on business connected with his wife's estates, and the administration of the Government *pro tem.*, conformably to the King's instructions, fell upon Colonel Abraham de Peyster, senior member of the Council. Captain Nanfan shortly afterwards returned to New York and remained in charge of affairs until the arrival of Edward Hyde, styled by courtesy Lord Cornbury, who was appointed to fill the vacancy occasioned by Bellomont's death.

Such an eminent authority as the historian Macauley, after a brief review of Bellomont's career, declares that he was a man " of eminently fair character, upright, courageous, and independent." In this opinion it would be impossible for a conscientious student of history not to concur. Beset in his administration by difficulties the most harassing, maligned and misrepresented to the Home Government, lacking the support of the most of those in the Province who belonged to the wealthy and aristocratic classes, and conscious that these latter were continually intriguing to secure his disgrace and removal, he yet never was tempted to swerve from his duty, which he made superior to every consideration. And there is no doubt, had his life been spared, that he would have succeeded in carrying out to a successful ending, the numerous reforms in the conduct of colonial affairs which had been so flatteringly and confidently entrusted to his management by the King; and that his wise policy for improving, developing and harmonizing the interests of the colonies, would have been productive of the happiest results.

In conclusion, I have only to add that a careful study of the history of the period, has convinced me that Lord Bellomont was

COL. ABRAHAM DE PEYSTER.

MRS. COL. ABRAHAM DE PEYSTER.

persistently maligned and abused, solely because he had an eye to the public service and not to individual advancement. Strange to say, his enemies were to be found among all classes, a fact which, to my mind, however, determines his great honesty and independence of character. Those engaged in illegal trade hated him, because he was not to be bribed or cajoled into tolerating the least infraction of laws. The merchants were also his enemies, because he would not violate his obligation of office and wink at their evasions of the Acts of Trade. All opposed to Leisler and Milborne were against him, because he carried out the Act of Parliament ordering that justice be done their memory. Even the greater part of the clergy were arrayed against him : those of the Dutch Church, because he would not tolerate the iniquitous conduct of Dellius ; and those of the English Church, because he would not alienate a portion of the estate attached to the Governor's residence. Thus it will be seen the private interests of a large class were opposed to the law; and Bellomont, as the representative of the law, and its faithful administrator, was reprobated and vilified by that class.

It must not be thought from this that he had no friends and adherents among the colonists. On the contrary, his cordiality and fair-dealing won for him the esteem of all right-minded persons; and by them he was both appreciated and respected. His only weapon in dealing with his enemies was the truth. To him is eminently applicable the famous lines of Horace :

> " *Integer vitæ scelerisque purus*
> *Non eget Mauri jaculis, neque arcu*
> *Nec venenatis gravida sagittis*
> *Fusce, pharetra :*"

thus admirably translated by the Reverend Doctor Francis :—

> *The Man, who knows not guilty Fear,*
> *Nor wants the Bow, nor pointed Spear ;*
> *Nor needs, while innocent at Heart,*
> *The Quiver, teeming with the poison'd Dart.*

ERRATA.

Page 6, fourth line............................ for *Dwitwich* read Droitwich.
" " last line............................ " *indisputed* " indisputable.
" 7, fifteenth line........................... " *who* " which,
" 9, thirtieth line.......................... " *following* " following.
" 10, third line............................ " *Willliam* " William.
" 12, fourteenth line................. .... " *twarted* " thwarted.
" 13, eleventh line, after " Holmes " should be a proper marginal reference, and at foot of page a note, giving as authority, Gen. Cust's *Lives of the Warriors*, Vol. II, p. 482.
" 13, [Note] * should read *The Old Streets of New York under the Dutch*, by James W. Gerard.
" 14, [Note] * should read Davies' *History of Holland*.
" 16, third and sixth lines.................. for *Dominic* read Dominie.
" 17, twentieth line....................... " *latter* " later.
" 19, eleventh line......................... " *gereral* " general.
" 21, twenty-third line............... ...... " *out* " on.
" 22, seventh line.......................... " *Colombus* " Columbus.
" " thirty-fourth line...................... " *whith* " with.
" 25, [Notes] *, †, ‡, §..................... " *Kidd* " "A full Account of the Proceedings in relation to Capt. Kidd ; in two Letters Written by a person of Quality to a Kinsman of the Earl of Bellomont in Ireland. [London ; MDCCI.]
" 27, first line.... .... for *Oxford* read Orford.
" " twenty-ninth line..................... " *have* " have had.
" 30, twenty-ninth line..................... " *French* " French.
" 31, fourteenth line...................... " *unsually* " unusually.
" 34, twenty-ninth line.............. .... " *Governer* " Governor.
" 49, first line............................ " *Oxford,* " Orford.
" 50, third line............................ " *chafing* " chafing.
" 53, eighteenth line...................... " *his* " is.
" 54, twenty-sixth line..................... " *England* " New England.
" " thirtieth line......................... " *Bishops* " Bishop.
" 55, first line............................ " *than that* " than of that.
" " sixteenth line......................... " *obtaind* " obtained.
" " twenty-eighth line.................... " *Classes* " Classis.
" " twenty-ninth line..................... " *Bishops* " Bishop.

APPENDIX.

LETTERS FROM THE EARL OF BELLOMONT

TO

COLONEL ABRAHAM DE PEYSTER.

[Originals in the possession of the New York Historical Society.]

BOSTON, *the 9th of Jan'y,* [16] *'99.*

SR. I have yours of the 26th of last month, and desire you will be as good as your word in getting the four hatts made, and sent to *Barbadoes.*

I desire you will deliver the Inclosed Letter to Mr. LATHAM with your own hand, and pray Incourage him all you can to proceed upon cutting the Ship Timber that I have directed him. I have got the sizes and scantlings of such Timber as will be proper for the King's use, and have now sent an acc't of them to Mr. LATHAM. You will do well to Injoyn Mr. LATHAM to take speciall care to cut none but such as is principall and choice Timber, and to do it as cheaply as he can reasonably afford it. It behooves you to take some pains with LATHAM, so that the King may be compensated for putting the ship Fortune upon him, which I am in some apprehension the Ministers will resent as a misconduct in the Lt. Governor and Councill of N. York; and there is no way of repairing the King, but by sending him that Ship's Loading of choice Timber, and at a cheap rate.

As to the report of my Lord CORNBERY'S* coming over Governor, if it were true I should be very easy; but I do not at all believe it, the more for its comeing from DELLIUS, who, we all know, has a notable Talent at lying.

* Lord CORNBURY succeeded 3d May, 1702, after the death of BELLOMONT.

I cannot draw Bills of Exchange for money in Engl'd till I have advice that the arrear Due to the souldiers is received. There came a ship in here from England on Sunday last, after twelve weeks' passage, but I had not one letter by her. The Master tells me that Capt. MASON, Master of the ship BELLOMONT, had severall packets for me ; he was sailing out of the Downs, along with this ship, but the wind chopping about, he fears Capt. MASON was forced back again.

I am heartily glad of your good Luck, in your ships comeing in from the *Madeiras*, at a time when there is such a scarcity of wine at N. York.

I desire you will make some safe bargains w'th Mr. LATHAM, and furnish him with money. I shall by next post write to Coll. CORTLAND to pay you all the arrears of my salary. I wish you would take a copy of my Letter to Mr. LATHAM, which I have not time now to send you. My Service to Madm. D– PEYSTER.   I am

Your humble Servant,

BELLOMONT.

BOSTON, *the 22nd Jan'y.* [16] '99.

SR. I have got the gout in my right hand, and cannot yet write to you my Self. The Pipe of wine last come from the *Madeiras*, must be delivered to my Cousin NANFAN, but the Box of Sweets * is a present from Mr. BOLTON, the Consul, to my Wife ; therefore I desire you will send it by the first opportunity to her.

I recommended your business with Mr. VAN SWEETING to my Lord Chancellor and Mr. Secretary VERNON, and drew up a state of your case with my own hand, as well as I could, and sent to each of them ; but then your freinds that solicits your business in London, must apply to my Lord Chancellor and Mr. Secretary, with great Caution and discretion ; for men of their upright character will not care to be solicited in a matter of that nature. Our last ship went for England about Ten days ago, so that I cannot have an opportunity of writing again about that business of yours till Spring.

I desire you will not faile to take a speciall care about the Ship Timber, which I writ to you of last post, for I look upon my Reputation to be much concerned in that matter.

I send you a Copy of Mr. BOLTON'S Letter to me, that you may see what

* The word is doubtful.

he writes, and what he Challenges as due to him upon the Balance of the account.

I hear the Jacobite party in N. York have named a new Governor, before the King has thought fit to name one; and I am also told they lay Waggers that I shall not go any more to N. York; but for all that, I desire you will bespeak me Two pipes of good ale and Two pipes of small beer at Albany or Schenectady, which I would have laid in at N. York, against my goeing thither. Pray charge the man you bespeak it of to boyle it very well, and to make it as good as possibly he can.

I have writ to Coll. CORTLANDT, by the post, to pay you what money is due to me of my salary, which I desire you will call to him for. My Service to Madam DE PEYSTER.

I am, your humble Servant,

BELLOMONT.

BOSTON, *the 5th of Feb'y,* [16] '99.

SR. I have your letter of the 22d of last month, but have rec'd no Letter from Mr. LATHAM, as you made me expect, by this post. The Scantlings of Ship Timber I mentioned in my Letter to him, are for a first-rate Man-of-War. If he cannot get Timber of so large a size, I would have him get as near those sizes as he can, for, the bigger and larger, the better. If he does not make haste to cut the Timber, he will lose the proper season of the year; therefore, I beg of you to hasten him all that ever you can, and give him Incouragement that I will be very kind to him if he uses me faithfully and well in the Ship Timber.

I have writ very pressingly to Coll. CORTLANDT to pay you my full arrear of Salary, which I hope he will do, especially if you Dun him a little for it.

If the other Hatter you mention will make the four Hatts I bespoke as well as YARRINGTON, I shall be satisfied that he make them.

The Two Merchant Ships that have Letters for me from England, are not yet arrived, but the advice Man-of-War, a 4th rate, Capt. WYNN, Commander arrived here last Saturday, in six weeks, from Portsmouth, and brought me orders from the King to send home all the Pyrates and their Effects. The Ministers continue to write to me with great Kindness, and tell me the King is very well pleased with my administration in my Governments. If the angry Gentlemen of N. York have their Intelligence from better hands than the King's Ministers, or of a Later Date than the 10th of last December, then I shall believe they are very deep in the secrets of the Cabinet; and if they can prevail by their Interest to make a new Governour of New York, with all my heart what please the King shall please me. Our Service to Madam DE PEYSTER.

I am,

Your humble Servant,

BELLOMONT.

BOSTON, *the 19th Feb'y, 1699.*

SIR. I find the Letters which I writ to England about your business, are rec'd, for I have answer to them.

I am very thankful to you for your care in Imploying Mr. LATHAM to provide the Ship Timber. I desire you will continue your care in Incouraging of him to the speedy and exact performance of that service, wherein you can never oblige me more as long as you live. If I imploy any body at New York to go home Master of the ship Fortune, it shall be that SYMMONS that you mention, because you recommend him; but I would not absolutely engage myself to him as yet, because possibly some reason may offer in the meantime why he may not be so proper a man for such a Trust.

I desire you will take care to send the Inclos'd to Mr. BOLTON, the Consul of the *Madeiras;* and that you will also send the money he charges in his acc't as due by me to him. I have sent to him for three pipes of wine—one whereof I have bespoke to be white Madeira. I desire you will give the Master of your ship particular charge of my pipes of wine, and that you will send as much money in Bits* as will pay for those three pipes.

My Cousin NANFAN will show you part of a Letter from one of the King's Ministers to me, by this Man-of-War, w'ch I have already copied exactly from the said Letter. I do assure you I have had Letters by the same ship from almost all the Ministers, full of expressions of kindness, and approving of and Commending up my Administration in my Governments.

My Service I pray to Madam DE PEYSTER.

I was yesterday on horseback, and rid four or five miles, but am yet weak, especially in my hands, so that I cannot write without Trouble.

I am,

Your humble Servant,

BELLOMONT.

---

* *Bits*— Probably PISTAREENS (Spanish and West Indian), of which there were as many as a half dozen (or more) kinds, bearing different dates and varying slightly in value—from 16 to 18 cents U. S. currency.

BOSTON, *the 17th of March*, [16] '99.

SIR. I am heartily vex'd to understand from my Cousin NANFAN that LATHAM has not yet cut the Timber I directed, for now the Spring is so forward that they will perceive, when it comes into England, that the Timber was not cut in the proper season. This will be reckoned a fault in me, that after I have given an account home of my design of sending that Ship Loaden w'th Ship Timber, I should come off so poorly as to send what is not good or in season. I fear this neglect in LATHAM is not to be retriev'd.

I shall not venture to order the money you writ about in your last letter for bringing stores from England formerly, till I go to New York, and then advise with the Council about it.

I have writ to my Cousin NANFAN to appoint Mr. WALTERS Judge in your stead *pro hac vice.** I am quite out of money here, and must draw on Coll. COURTLANDT for 50£, unless you have received my Salary from him. Our Service to Madam DE PEYSTER.　　　　I am,

　　　　　　　　　　　　　　　　　　Your humble Servant,

Coll. DE PEYSTER.　　　　　　　　　　　　　　BELLOMONT.

PESCATAQUA, *3d Aug.*, [16] '99.

SIR. I hope this Letter will find you safely arriv'd at York, where I wish you may meet your family and friends in good health.

I desire you will not faile to send me a copy of the French Lady's letter to her Paramour, Mr. DELLIUS, about the big belly she lays to his charge ; and, if it be possible to recover the original Letter, I desire you will get it for me, and send it by the first post. I intend, next post, to write to Coll. COURTLANDT, to pay you the arrear of my Salary, and also the growing Income thereof monethly, as it becomes due. I have not time now to write to him. I wish you would tell Mr. LEISLER that I cannot move the King to get his father's debt order'd to be paid, for want of GOVERNEUR'S and other people's testimony, on oath, that they saw Capt. LEISLER'S bookes and that there was such a sum due, as Dr. STAATS and GOVERNEUR told me ; but the sum they mention'd I have forgot. Let this be done Immediately, if they are able to Swear to it ; it must be drawn up handsomely, that I may transmit it to England.

I desire you will find out some honest, able ship carpenter at York, to send along with RYER SCHERMERHOORN, to view the woods on Mr. DELLIUS'S

---

* "*Pro hac vice.*"—" For this term," or, " For this time ;" *i. e.* " For this occasion."
Col. DE PEYSTER and ROBERT WALTERS were Puisne Judges of the Supreme Court.

biggest Grant,* and to bring me an exact account whether there be any Pine or fir Trees big enough or long enough for Masts for the King's ships of War, from 30 inches to 48 inches in diameter, and whether there grow any quantity, and how convenient for a water carriage. That is, whether they grow near the river, that they may be floated down the river to York. He must be very particular in his account and very exact, that I may send it to England; and I would have him also bring an account what other sorts of well grown Timber Trees of oak or other trees he meets with there, and he must go over all that Land to view the woods, which I would have him put into writing. Therefore, the man you send ought to know how to write. There was also some other part of the Country which RYER SCHERMERHOORN, and, I thinke, the Mayor of Albany, told me of, where they said there grew good masts for ships. I desire you will appoint the Carpenter to go thither along with RYER; also, I leave it with you to make the bargain with the Carpenter, and I will perform it with him; and if he wants money to bear his charges, I desire you will advance it, and stop it out of my Salary. Pray send the account as it stands between you and me. I desire you will take all possible care to preserve the ship Fortune, and I will send her to England, next Spring, with naval stores to the King. Let me hear from you every post. Myne, with my wife's kind Service to your selfe and Madam DE PEYSTER.

I am   Your very affectionate Servant,

BELLOMONT.

I have receiv'd your Letter from Boston. I desire to know when the next ship goes to England, that I may send the pipe of wine.

———

BOSTON, 21 Aug. [16] 99.

SIR. I am very glad of your safe arrival at York, and I must tell you we misse you here, where you are in the favor and good opinion of every body. If Dr. STAATS and Mr. GOVERNEUR'S† memories are too short in respect to the debt due to Capt. LEISLER, I know not which way to move the King in behalf of Mr. LEISLER, for, unlesse the debt can be ascertained, it would be most ridiculous for me to ask the King to refund to the heir of Capt. LEISLER a debt of I know not what sum. Therefore I advise you to call Mr. LEISLER,

———

* See SMITH's *History of New York*, page 159, Edition (Albany) in 1 Vol. of 1814.

† ABRAHAM GOUVERNEUR, Member from Orange County; married Gov. LEISLER's daughter, the widow of MILBORNE.

Dr. STAATS, and Mr. WALTERS and Mr. GOVERNEUR together, and see what they can say to refresh one another's memory in that matter; otherwise it will be Impossible for me to do Mr. LEISLER the Service I am desirous to do him.

I would willingly send my pipe of wine to England, but JEFFERS is so Crosse a fellow, and not my friend, that I am not willing to venture it by him, least he should play tricks with it out of spite to me: but, where there is a good opportunity, I will desire the favor of you to have it shipp'd, and sent to England. My Cousin, NANFAN, has the key to the Cellar where the pipe of wine is; it was left by JOHN, my butler, with ROBERT, the Coachman's Wife. You may Call to 'em for it, and send the wine when you see convenient; but I believe the pipe must be fill'd up, which I desire may be done with good wine. When the ship is almost ready to saile let me know, that I may write a letter, to the person I send the pipe of wine to in England.

I desire you will let me know pr next post whether the battery which Coll. FLETCHER sold, or granted away to EBENEZER WILSON, be entirely built on in N. York, and whose land it was he made batteries on in the war time. Mr. LEISLER I believe was one, and I think a quaker another—GEORGE HEATHCOTE is the Quaker's name, as I thinke. But, pray, inform your selfe of this particularly, and let me know.

You must by all means get me that Letter from the woman in Canada to DELLIUS, and send it me by next post, if it be possible, for 't will be of great use to me.

I am not at all pleased with your present Sheriffe, DE RYMER.* I hear he returns such Juries as do the King all the wrong in the world, upon all the Tryals of unlawful things and goods. I know not whether I have reason to like GOVERNEUR better than DE RYMER. The not sending home an agent from the Assembly to withstand the Indeavors of BAYARD DELLIUS, and all the knaves of that party, was the foolishest step that was ever made. I told Dr. STAATS enough of it, but could not get him to apprehend the Importance of it; and, it seem'd to me, that Volatile Speaker, GOVERNEUR, acted in concert with his Predecessor, and was false to his party. New York is an unhappy place, that there is not better choice of men to serve the King and their Country. My wife fell very ill on the road between Pescattaqua and this place; but, I thank God, is somewhat better. Our kind Service to Madam DE PEYSTER; mine to Dr. STAATS, Mr. WALTERS, and your brother. Pray let me hear from you what passes at York; and, be assured that, I am,

Your very affectionate friend and serv't,

BELLOMONT.

---

* This must be DE RIEMER. See V. H. N. Y., page 233.

Mr. SCHERMERHOORN, whom I writ to, to go and view some trees fit for masts for the King's ships, and send me word where they grew, and of what bigness they were, has answered my Letter, but tells me not where the trees grow, only says there are a good store, and large enough for the King's use. He desires I would grant him and the Mayor of Albany the Land where they grow, w'ch is 6 miles long and 2 broad, which is making a bargain with the King, and not dealing candidly with me. Pray, chide him and the Mayor of Albany for their disrespect to the King, and disingenueity to me. Besides, I have complain'd to the King of Coll. FLETCHER'S extravagant Grant's of Lands—and shall I commit the same fault and absurdity my selfe, that I have accus'd FLETCHER? Pray, let me know whether Dr. STAATS is likely to prevail with LUPARDUS and NUCELLA, to write to the Classis of Amsterdam and the Dutch Ministers in London, to prevent DELLIUS'S ill designs and Lyings. Pray, send me a barrel of the best flour by the first sloop.

BOSTON, *28th Aug.*, [16] '99.

SIR. I thank you kindly for your Care in Imploying LATHAM to go and view the woods along with Mr. SCHERMERHOORN. Mr. LEISLER * being here, I will make up of Dr. STAATS and Mr. GOVERNEUR'S affidavits, for his Interest and Service, and will send them to such hands in England as will make, I hope, a right use of them.

I have not now Time to look over your account, though I am under no doubt with you—(having an entire opinion of your sincerity and uprightnesse)—nor yet to order Coll. COURTLANDT to satisfie my debt to you; but by next post you may expect it.

I will not faile to write to the Ministers, in whom I have an Interest, in your behalf; and will transmit them a state of your Case, exactly as you have now sent it to me. I am now engaged in preparing packets for England, to send by a ship that will go the end of this week or beginning of the next; and then you shall not be forgot. My wife and I present our kind service to Madam DE PEYSTER. She bids me tell you the Letter Madam DE PEYSTER was to write to her is forgot, and she upbraids you for deluding her w'th such false hopes.   I am,

Your very affectionate friend and servant,

BELLOMONT.

* Son of the "remarkable" and deservedly distinguished Gov'r, JACOB LEISLER, executed for treason in 1691, whose innocence was subsequently established, the attainder reversed, and his property restored to his family through the exertions of his son—by whom the loyalty of his father and of his brother-in-law, MILBORNE, and the machinations of their enemies, were plainly made manifest.

[On the back of the letter is the following:]

Mr. WEAVER is certainly Collector of N. York, and has the King's Commission for it, as Sr. JOHN STANLEY writes me a word in a Letter I rec'd from him this last week; and Mr. WEAVER writes in his last Letter he had kissed the King's hand for it, and had got the King's Warrant for preparing his Commission under the Great seal of England. I hope you have prevail'd w'th Dr. STAATS, and those that have an Influence on Mr. NUCELLA and LUPARDUS, to get them to write to the Classis of Amsterdam to defeat DELLIUS'S knavish designs. The LEISLER party had done well to have subscrib'd Certificates against DELLIUS, as his friends did for him, and to have sent them to me.

———

BOSTON, *4th Sept.,* [16] '99.

SIR. I cannot perform my promise of Looking over your account as yet, for I am Ingaged at present, and have been so all this last week, in writing packets or volumes of Letters to England by a ship that pretends she stays for me.

I writ to my Cousin NANFAN, last post, to Let the City of N. York have ye stones of the old bastion or batteries To build their Town-house.

I am not dissatisfied with the Sheriffe, since my Cousin NANFAN and you vouch so for his honesty; but he should have taken more care of BUCKMASTER.

I have writ to my Cousin NANFAN, this post, my reasons why it will not be fitt to Continue the same Mayor and Sheriffe another year for the city of N. York.

As soon as you receive the original, or a Copy of the Letter to DELLIUS from the French woman at Canada, I desire you will not fail to send it To

Your very affectionate Servant,

BELLOMONT.

Our Service I pray to Madam DE PEYSTER.

Mr. LEISLER tells me an ugly story of Mr. GRAHAM'S design of Cheating him of a house-plot at N. York. I desire you will send for Mr. WALTERS privately, and advise him to Caution old Mrs. LEISLER (with whom her son has left a Generall Letter of Attorney) not to part with that piece of ground to GRAHAM, nor anything else. That man will undo himself with his knavish Tricks. One would thinke he has guilt enough on his head, for being the Principall author of the murther of LEISLER and MILBURN; but, it seems, bathing his hands in the blood of the Father is not enough, but he will also cheat the son. I am content that you show this Letter to Mr. WALTERS; and pray get him to send me affidavit of Mr. GRAHAM's Insinuations to his Father, LEISLER, and himselfe, to procure their Interest to be chosen a member of the Assembly; w'ch they were prevail'd with to do, and afterwards he became LEISLER's and MILBURN's mortall Enemy. This account Mr. WALTERS told me once or twice.

Dr. STAATS also told me how he was affronted, and threatened by a Papist in the field, when the Election was of members to serve in New York, in that very Assembly that worried Mr. LEISLER and MILBURN to death, under the conduct of Mr. GRAHAM. Let me also have Dr. STAATS' affidavit of that; and some proof of Maj. TREADWELL's imprisonment to hinder either his being Chose, or his sitting in Assembly after he was Chose. If it be possible, let me have these evidences next post.

BOSTON, *Sept. 9th,* [16] *'99.*

SIR. I have receiv'd yours of the 4th Inst., and will not faile to write to England ab't your affair with VAN SWEETON w'th this packet, w'ch I am to send away within 4 or 5 days.

I am very sorry I have not the Letter to DELLIUS to send home. I desire you will speak to Mr. WALTERS to deliver you upon oath what was transacted between Mr. GRAHAM and him at the time GRAHAM prevail'd w'th Capt. LEISLER and him to make an interest for GRAHAM's being chose to the Assembly, that press'd Coll. SLAUGHTER to take away the lives of Capt. LEISLER and Mr. MILBURN, as I writ to you in my last Letter. And, pray, get Dr. STAATS' affidavit, as I desir'd in that Letter. 'T is wonderfull to me that Dr. STAATS and the rest of LEISLER'S Party have not, in all this time, got counter-subscriptions, sign'd by their party, at Albany, against DELLIUS, as the other party got subscriptions in favor of DELLIUS. They are just the people that WILL. NICHOLS paints STAATS to be, in his pamphlet, Impenetrable B———. [blockheads?]

When you hear any news from SCHERMERHOORN ab't the Trees for masts, pray let me know it. My wife's and my Service to Madam DE PEYSTER.

I am,

Your affectionate friend and servant,

BELLOMONT.

I have writ to Coll. COURTLANDT to pay you my arrear of Salary, and for ye time to come to pay it to you monthly, as it grows due.

Coll. DE PEYSTER.

———

BOSTON, *the 30th Oct.*, [16] '99.

SIR. I desire you will immediately send for Mr. LATHAM, the ship Carpenter, and Ingage him to set about Cutting and Squaring such a quantity of Ship Timber as will load the Ship Fortune against the Spring, when I will send her so loaden to Portsmouth, in England, for the use of the King's Navy. The question will be, whether LATHAM be well affected and honest, and will cut such Timber as is choice Timber. The four sorts w'ch I understand are fitted to be sent to England, are knees, planks, beams, and wale pieces. The next best thing to the cutting of principall Choice Timber, is the doing of it Cheap—wherein I desire you will contrive all the ways you can think of, for my credit. If 3 or 4 souldiers will be useful to Mr. LATHAM to help in felling of Trees, my Cousin NANFAN, upon sight of this Letter, will order so many of them, if so many can be found that will or can work; and I will allow such souldiers 4 shills. per week over and above their present subsistence. Pray, take more than ordinary pains to agree w'th LATHAM at as cheap a rate as possibly you can. My wife's and my kind Service to Madam DE PEYSTER.

I am,

Yr. very affect. friend and servant,

BELLOMONT.

[On the back of the Letter is the following:]

I will not fail to recommend you to England, for the supplying the frigat at N. York; and I hope ere long to Imploy you in a businesse that will be five times more profitable than that. Pray, write me word, next post, what agreement LATHAM and you are like to come to. I would have you acquaint my Cousin NANFAN w'th the steps you make in that matter, and take his advice in every p'ticular ab't it.

I hope you have taken care to return another 100£ to Mr. PALMER, in beaver skins, or logwood, or something; and if you have not done it, I desire you will not faile to do it by next ship, and send me word of it with the master's and ship's name, that I may give Mr. PALMER's advice of it from hence.

[*This is another Letter—date gone.*]

I have rec'd yours of the 8th Inst., and have writ to my Cousin NANFAN, to stand by and support LATHAM in cutting and bringing away the Timber. I have letters from England by MASON, but the dates so stale that the news and accounts must be so too. The Ministers seem pleas'd with the act of Assembly of N. York for vacating the extravagant Grants of Lands. We have no news of Mr. Goodwin's receit of the 50£ you remitted to London for my wife. Pray, let me know if your Correspondent has given you any account of paying that money.

I have writ to Coll. COURTLANDT, this post, to quicken him in paying you all that is due of my salary—tho' he has promis'd, in his letter, this post, to do it out of the first money he receives. In his account sent out a month ago, he charges me with 300£, which I order'd to be paid to Coll. SCHUYLER, for victualling, soon after coming into that province; but I have now writ to my Cousin NANFAN, to p'cure an order of Council for placing that debt on the Revenue, there being no reason in the world I should pay it out of my salary. Therefore, there will be 300£ more for you to receive for me—only that I am willing to Lend my Co. NANFAN 50£ of it. I desire you will not faile to . . . . for charging that sum . . . . . . and when that's done, to solicite Coll. COURTLANDT for the payment of that, and all the rest of my arrear of salary to you.

My wife desires yours and Madam DE PEYSTER's care in Looking after the necklace of pearl. She has sent you a role of Tobacco lately, sent me from Virginia, by Coll. JENNINGS, w'ch she hopes will prove as sweet-scented as any you have smoak'd this long time. 'T is deliver'd to one TELLER, the master of a sloop, which is to sail the first fair wind to N. York.

Pray, take care about providing suitable goods for the Indians, against my going to Albany, as I desired you in my last. Our affectionate service to Madam DE PEYSTER.

I am your affectionate friend, and humble servant,

BELLOMONT.

Pray, do not fail to speak to my Co. NANFAN, to order Coll. COURTLANDT to pay you the price of the ship Nassau, w'ch Mr. GRAHAM gave his opinion belonged wholly to me, as being a wreck, and Mr. NEWTON is of the same opinion here. There's no reason Coll. COURTLANDT should keep the money all this while in his hands, and I perceive he would willingly to the end of the Chapter.

Coll. HAMILTON writes to a person in this Town that the faction . . . k desire that DE . . . . not return to Albany. Pray, let me know how you feel by that piece of news.

———

BOSTON, *the 24th*.

SIR. I have rec'd, this post, your Letters of the 8th and 18th Inst., and am glad you have Imployed Mr. LATHAM in Cutting the Ship Timber, and hope he will perform that service according to my expectation. I writ last post to the Lieut.-Governor, to appoint Mr. WALTERS Judge of the Superior Court.

I am heartily glad of your victory agt. VAN SWEETEN in England. I am also glad of your two ships coming laden from the *Madeiras*, w'ch will supply new York plentifully w'th wine; and I hope you will find your account largely therein.

I desire you will let me know what you take to be the Cause of the present scarcity of money in N. York. It would make one believe merchants there send it to England in specie, as the merchants here do.

I have writ, this post, again, to Coll. COURTLANDT, to pay you all the arrears of my salary. He shall find, in a little time, that I know when I am ill us'd, for I can take away when I please the benefit he has of furnishing the Fort with wood, and other things, and paying workmen, w'ch I believe he makes more than ordinary advantage of, and also of victualling the Companies —and of this last article . . . . . a good advantage, when the subsistence is paid in England. I am now in a way of making that matter certain, so that the victuallers shall, for the time to come, receive their money duly.

My wife presents her thanks and service to Madam DE PEYSTER, for her kind Letter. She has a pain in her head, or she would answer it this post: she desires by all means Madam DE PEYSTER will be so kind as to secure the pearl necklace for her, if it be good and Cheap.

I draw on Coll. COURTLANDT, this post, for 56£ 5s., by bill of exchange, payable to JOSEPH BUENO, the Jew, at ten days' sight. I wish you would watch whether COURTLANDT be carefull to save my credit. Perhaps he may be such a brute as to let my credit suffer, and not accept my bill: but I will then Immediately turn him out of all. I dare not meddle with a farthing of the 2,000£ tax till I have the King's leave. I am quite out of money. I hope to see you at N. York the latter end of June. My service to Madam DE PEYSTER. I conclude.

Your very affectionate Friend and Servant,

BELLOMONT.

Against next post, I will examine Coll. COURTLANDT'S account of my salary, which I have not yet had time to do.

———

BOSTON, *the 5th April, 1700.*

SIR. I receiv'd not yours of the 25th of last month till this day—the post having been stopped four or five days on the way hither by the bad weather.

I am very thankfull for your kindness, in supplying me with the Two 50£ bills of exchange ; but having drawn last post on Coll. COURTLANDT for 50£, I shall have occasion but for one of the Bills, and do now return you t'other.

I am glad you write me word that Mr. LATHAM is proceeding in cutting the Ship Timber, which I desire you will Incourage him in, for I set my heart much on that matter.

I have directed a message to be carried to the 5 Nations, by Coll. SCHUYLER, Mr. LIVINGSTON and Mr. HANSON, and JOHN BAPTIST VAN EPP is to go Interpreter with them. They are to go no further than to the Onondaga's Castle, and are to send my message to the other Nations by some trusty Indians. They have my instructions, in writing, what to say to the Indians, and how to behave themselves in every respect. I have appointed all the Sachems of the 5 Nations to meet me at Albany on the 10th day of next August, and the messengers are to tell them that I intend them then a good present. I desire you will keep this private a while, tho' long it will not be a secret at Yorke, because I have writ to the Commiss'ers at Albany of my design. I wish you would advise me, too, how I may secure a quantity of such woolen clothes as are fit for the Indians, viz : shrowds and dresses, &c., and not pay so extravagant rates for them, as I did the last time I went to Albany, and there must be Linen for shirts for them too. I would gladly have you and Mr. LIVINGSTON concern'd in furnishing those things, provided I may be reasonably used, and I will undertake to pay you in 3 months' time. I intend as good a present to the Indians as ever was yet made them, and from thence you may take your measures as to the quantity you are to provide. I am told those woolends may be had 20 per cent. cheaper than at York; but I hope you will take such a course, as I may not be abus'd in the price. I would employ you singly in the affair, but that I am obliged to Mr. LIVINGSTON, and would not willingly put any slight upon him. Besides, I believe I must lodge at his house at Albany.

We are in fear that the ship commanded by MASON and HORTON, and the brigantine by JONES, are all three lost.

Pray, give my service to your brother, the late Mayor, and to Dr. STAATS, Mr. WATERS and Mr. GOVERNEUR. Tell Mr. GOUVERNEUR I rec'd his letter and news, and thank him for it, but have not time to write to him.

I desire you will Inquire whether there has been any news at York of Mr. LEISLER'S arrivall in England. I sent a packet to England by him, to the Ministers—but have not since heard of him or from him.

Let me know if it be True if Mr. HUNGERFORD is married to Mistress BOND.

My wife desires the favor of Madam DE PEYSTER, to buy her the pearl necklace, if they be good and reasonably cheap. So, w'th our kind service to her, I conclude.

Your affectionate friend and humble servant,

BELLOMONT.

———

BOSTON, *the 12th of May, 1700.*

SIR. I had not time to write to you last post, to tell you I receiv'd yours of the 29th of last month, w'th 3 papers inclosed, viz : a bill of loading signed MATHIAS DE HART, another signed JOHN VAN BRUGH, and a copy of Coll. COURTLANDT'S account of the price of the ship Nassau.

Yours of the 6th inst. I rec'd last night. I desire you will deliver the Inclosed letter to Capt. EVERTSON, for the Governor of Kickoverall. When I come to York, it will be time enough to endenize Capt. EVERTSON, and so tell him. I had a letter from Mr. GOVERNEUR about itt this post.

I am glad the new Town-house is so far advanced. I fear by Mr. LATHAM'S stay so long in the woods, he will make that Ship Timber I bespoke very chargeable, w'ch will spoil the good grace of the matter.

Our kind service to Madam DE PEYSTER. I am,

Your affectionate friend and servant,

BELLOMONT.

Dr. STAATS writes Coll. ROMER word that SPENCER is come from England, and says he heard FLETCHER* say he would have me out of my Governments, tho' it should cost him 10,000£. Pray, let me know the truth of it, but make the inquiry as privately as you can.

DE RIMER, the late Sheriffe, and Mr. GOUVERNEUR, have plaid the fool extremely, for taking such a foolish bond for SHELLEY'S appearance. I believe I shall be directed from England to prosecute them both for putting such a fraud upon the King, for it can passe under no better a name.

BOSTON, *the 8th of June, 1700.*

SIR. I am glad of your safe return home from your circuit. I have had no letters from the Ministers by the two Ships lately come from London, except one from my Lord Chancellor, and two or three from particular friends. It seems Mr. WEAVER sent the Ministers packets by JEFFERS, to N. York, who is, I hope, arriv'd there by this time. I am afraid LATHAM will have made that Timber he is about very chargeable, which will spoil my design in a great measure.

I am quite out of paper, and this town affords none that is good. Our kind Service to Madam DE PEYSTER.

I am your affectionate friend and Servant,

BELLOMONT.

Pray, call on Mr. CLARKSON for my fees, and receive them for me. I believe I shall be forced to find another Secretary, that has sense enough not to betray the Secrets of the Government. HUNGERFORD must have had notice of the writts for arresting, from CLARKSON.

BOSTON, *the 7th July, 1700.*

SIR. LATHAM'S account has frighted me—it seeming to me a most extravagant one. I can only tell you that Mr. PARTRIDGE, for 300£, loaded a ship of 260 Tons, at Pescattaway; and the ship Fortune, which is but of a 130 Ton, will, at this rate, take a load that will cost 306£. 6s. 2½d. I desire you

---

* Col. BENJAMIN FLETCHER, Governor of the Colony prior to BELLOMONT.

will forbear paying the money till I get to York, for I am not at all satisfied with LATHAM'S account, and his usage of me. I had better have had the timber provided at Pescattaway than have run the hazard of being so cheated, as I find I am like to be.

My wife and I are thankfule for your kind Invitation to your house, but we are Loath to be Troublesome to you, and therefore Intend to go directly to the Fort, and there take up our quarters. Our kind service to Madam DE PEYSTER.

I am your affectionate friend,

and humble servant,

BELLOMONT.

I intend to embark next Friday, God willing. I believe the Timber ought to be shipped out of hand.